D1627080

GOOD NEWS STUDIES

Consulting Editor: Robert J. Karris, O.F.M.

Volume 24

The Student's Guide
to the Gospels

James M. Reese, O.S.F.S.

A Michael Glazier Book
THE LITURGICAL PRESS
Collegeville, Minnesota

Cover by David Manahan, O.S.B.

A Michael Glazier Book published by The Liturgical Press

1	2	3	4	5	6	7	8	9

Library of Congress Cataloging-in-Publication Data

Reese, James M.
    The student's guide to the Gospels / James M. Reese.
      p. cm. — (Good news studies ; 24)
    "A Michael Glazier book."
    Includes bibliographical references and index.
    ISBN 0-8146-5689-7
    1. Bible. N.T. Gospels—Criticism, interpretation, etc.
I. Title. II. Series: Good news studies ; v. 24.
BS2555.2.R366   1991
226'.061—dc20
                                        91-35752
                                         CIP

Contents

Preface

Christians identify with the Gospels. They stand first in the New Testament, although they were not the first Christian writings. And the Church has maintained the custom of never celebrating the Eucharist without first reading from a gospel. These two facts illustrate why the Gospels embody the whole Christian tradition. Believers sense that there is no better path to the knowledge and love of Jesus than through the Gospels.

Yet many Christians do not feel at home with the Gospels. This struck me when I asked a group of adults in a continuing-education courses on the Gospels about their expectations. One woman said she was still searching to know Jesus. She had attended many courses on the New Testament but still did not feel she knew the Gospels.

This book addresses that situation. It focuses on two needs of believers, like those of that woman: (1) to become motivated to undertake a method that enables readers to dialogue with the Gospels themselves, and (2) to interiorize the message and spirit of the Gospels as the Church's authentic guide to the person and mission of Jesus.

To meet these needs, the first three chapters deal with the literary, structural, and rhetorical principles underlying the Synoptic Gospels. While studying these chapters, readers should be actively becoming acquainted with the Gospels of Matthew, Mark, and Luke. The rapid reading of these three Synoptics will clarify many of the points addressed in these three more-technical chapters. Repeated readings help believers see how these principles have a bearing on a real understanding of the gospel texts. The more familiar Christians become with all aspects of the Gospels by repeated readings, the easier it will be to appreciate their rhetorical features.

What has rhetoric to do with faith? Rhetoric is simply the art of persuasion, and the Gospels are works written to persuade readers to become disciples of Jesus. Rhetoric is not an extra in gospel study. It helps readers to visualize the Gospels as literary wholes and to feel the impact of their smaller units in light of that unity. This imaginative view is important because the Gospels are a type of literature much different from anything modern readers encounter today.

The remaining chapters encourage readers to dialogue with the Gospels in three ways: (1) Chapters 4, 5, and 7 explain the structure and theology of each Synoptic Gospel as a whole. This gives readers a sense of the unity, coherence, and emphasis of each one. (2) Special chapters are devoted to the four outstanding features of a gospel, namely, parables, miracles, the passion narratives, and the resurrection accounts. (3) The final chapter introduces readers to special features of John, The Fourth Gospel.

This flexible approach has been adopted to make this book useful in a variety of situations: classrooms, study clubs, prayer groups, individual study for beginners, even as a review for more advanced students.

All translations of gospel passages are my own. I have done this to gear them to the topic under discussion. My approach allows readers to compare passages with their favorite translation and to see how the text can be adapted to different readers and situations.

It is important for all students of the Gospels to read them over from time to time to refresh their memory about the characteristics of each. The evangelists brought different personalities and intentions to their writings of the story of Jesus. While affirming the whole New Testament as the good news, the Church is careful to maintain the integrity of each gospel presentation. This guarantees plurality to the Christian experience.

My thanks to the academic deans and to the chair and personnel committee of the Theology Department of St. John's University, New York City, for a research leave to complete this study guide of the four Gospels.

1

Introducing the Synoptic Gospels

The only comprehensive treatments of the earthly Jesus that have come down from the primitive Christian communities are the four Gospels. Three of these, the Gospels of Matthew, Mark, and Luke, present a similar picture of Jesus. They narrate his public career as less than a year long, beginning with his baptism by John. After gathering a small group of disciples, Jesus preached and performed mighty signs in Galilee.

Jesus then took his twelve hand-picked companions to Jerusalem, drove money changers out of the Jewish Temple, and preached briefly there. After being seized by Jewish authorities, he was crucified by Roman authority and rose from the dead on the third day. These three Gospels are called the "Synoptics" because their relationship can be seen "in a glance" (which is what the term means) when they are arranged side by side in parallel columns.

The Fourth Gospel is attributed to John. It deals with the ministry of Jesus, but in relation to Jewish feasts, especially three Passover celebrations. Some of its events are similar to accounts in the Synoptics, but its movement and presentation of the ministry of Jesus are quite different. The Fourth Gospel is treated separately, in chapter 11 of this book.

The first step in a systematic study of the Synoptic Gospels is to read each of them through as a religious narrative. That means reading them with the intention of entering into the spirit of Jesus as he goes about his mission. This approach empowers readers to experience and to judge how each author regarded Jesus. These three works are masterpieces of primary religious language. They are the outgrowth of a transforming religious experience of a community of believers.

This kind of reading of the Synoptics encourages followers of Jesus today to reflect on what is significant about his words and deeds for their lives and for their activity in continuing his saving mission in the world. The crucial element of such a reading is faith. Faith is a gift that opens readers to the Gospels as revelation, that is, as forms of God's saving power at work in Jesus. These small narratives were composed to be celebrated by Christian communities, not as apologetic documents aimed at converting Jews or Gentiles.

The second step in studying Gospels is to approach them as social documents, products of a special culture. They were written within believing communities and were meant primarily for the support of Christian worship-groups. When they were composed, printing did not exist. Each copy had to be written by hand. Any given community would have had a few copies, either in the form of scrolls, like the Hebrew Scriptures, or in the form that Christians preferred, book-type manuscripts, which were more easy to use.

The vast majority of original "readers" were actually hearers, following the story of Jesus in imagination, as the aside to the audience in Mark 13:14 indicates. A conscious attempt to identify with the way the original Christian readers received these Gospels is a necessary preparation for experiencing their power to transform human existence.

The Person of Jesus

The Synoptic Gospels came into existence and survived because the personality of Jesus was alive and appealing in early Christian communities. New believers wanted to know about him and to share his love with one another, as the prologue of Luke indicates (1:1-4). Jesus was a deeply religious person, one led by an overwhelming prophetic sense of mission to God's chosen people (Luke 9:51). He was totally dedicated to the will of his Father

(Matt 26:42; Luke 22:42). Often he sought communion with God in prayer, a practice emphasized in the Gospel of Luke.

Today Jesus would have been a media person, attracting attention by his rhetorical style, his striking images, his healing powers, and his penetrating vision of the kingdom of God, the plan that his Father had for the world. This sense of dedication prompted Jesus to proclaim his dedication to God publicly by seeking baptism from the fiery prophet John in the Jordan River. The Gospels record that the message opening the mission of Jesus was the joyful proclamation, "The kingdom of God has arrived" (Mark 1:15).

Jesus quickly gathered a group of followers and undertook the role of a wandering preacher "with nowhere to lay his head" (Matt 8:20). After a short period of success, his words and deeds brought him into conflict with the religious authorities of Judaism. Jesus was seized when he went to Jerusalem to celebrate the Passover and was put to death. This death did not put an end to the mission he began. In spite of rejection by the majority of his own people, a few of his followers believed that God had raised him from the dead. They soon convinced new members to join their fellowship, including one of its chief persecutors, the Pharisee Paul. Within two generations this community had spread throughout the Roman Empire and was recognized as having an identity distinct from traditional Judaism.

The Spirit of Jesus

What marked followers of Jesus, in addition to their initiation into the name or power of Jesus by baptism, was the outpouring of his personal Holy Spirit, who gave their lives new meaning and purpose. Often this presence burst forth by special signs, especially at baptism. The first written document of the Christian community, written by Paul to the Church at Thessalonica, warns members, "Do not extinguish the Spirit" (5:19). This dynamic presence propelled the community toward fearless unity in constructing a new model of mutual concern and hope. During this period of rapid expansion, it produced a small library of twenty-seven writings, which make up what Christians call the New Testament. These writings provide the universe of discourse, or symbolic world, that sustains all Christian thought and action.

As they branched out beyond the borders of Judea to set up worshiping communities in Hellenistic cities, the disciples of Jesus came to be identified as disciples of "the anointed one," or Christians (Acts 11:26). Outsiders recognized that their communities developed customs different from those of Jewish synagogues. These Christians reached out to all peoples as they struggled to create a world through which God was in Christ reconciling humanity to himself (2 Cor 5:18). Through their identity with the risen Christ, Christians addressed God as "Father" (Rom 8:15), just as the earthly Jesus had done (Mark 14:36). As possessors of his Spirit, believers looked forward to full and unending sharing in the glory of Jesus, who now reigns as risen Lord.

Christians proclaimed their experience of being saved in Jesus by celebrating the sacraments of baptism and the Eucharist, by developing new prayer forms, and by speaking in tongues under the influence of the Holy Spirit (1 Cor 14:4). Under the influence of the Apostle Paul, communities received Gentiles as equal partners in the new and eternal covenant sealed by the death and resurrection of Jesus. They struggled toward achieving the goal that Paul had expressed of abolishing all distinctions between Jew and Greek, slave and free, male and female, "For you are all one in Christ" (Gal 3:28).

Before it was necessary or even possible to compose gospels as we know them, the Christian community had to grow and face changes. It had to face up to an uncertain future in a hostile world. Christians could not sit back idly and expect the glorious kingdom preached by Jesus to manifest itself. That stage was in God's hands. Their task was to become Church, that is, a praying assembly of upright believers.

Members of the local communities were called upon to suffer in their efforts to imitate Jesus. Human knowledge begins with experience. Only those who suffer for Jesus "know him and the power of his resurrection and the sharing of his sufferings" (Phil 3:10). This example led to the spread of local Churches, described in schematic form in the Acts of the Apostles.

The earliest Christian writings, Paul's letters, scarcely mention the earthly life of Jesus. He never had any need to deal with it.

The Holy Spirit of the risen Jesus kept so active that early believers seldom looked back upon events of the earthly life of Jesus. Paul put his emphasis on the death and resurrection as the heart of God's saving work in Jesus. But second-generation Christians felt a need to know more about the earthly life of Jesus and sought out information.

Reasons for Composing Gospels

Christian communities founded by Paul maintained relations with the center of Jewish cult, the Temple of Jerusalem, where both Jesus and Paul had prayed, until it was destroyed by the Romans in 70 c.e. After that catastrophe Jewish cult had to be restructured along new lines. The rabbis who took the initiative created a new center of worship, no longer a place but the sacred writings of the tradition. For the first time the Jews established an official list, or canon, of Scripture, which we now call the Hebrew Bible.

As that reorganization of Jewish cult was taking place, the Christian movement also went through a period of significant change. Most of the original eyewitnesses and followers of the earthly Jesus were dead. The new generation of Christian leaders felt the need of authoritative accounts to preserve the apostolic experience. In that way, an inspired or normative presentation of the earthly Jesus was made available for future generations of believers.

These accounts of the mission of Jesus were eventually called gospels, ''good news.'' They still serve as the primary norm of the faith of every generation of Christians. During a whole generation, before the Gospels were written, traditions about the earthly Jesus were preserved in oral form by apostolic preachers and itinerant prophets. These early teachers devised narratives and discourses capable of instructing, guiding, encouraging, and admonishing Christian communities.

Very little can be said with certainty about the actual development of the tradition that grew up during the oral period. One helpful approach is found in the Dogmatic Constitution on Divine Revelation of Vatican II. That document, called *Dei verbum*, conveniently divides material about the ministry of Jesus into three stages:

Stage 1. The basis is the actual preaching and teaching of the earthly Jesus to his original audiences. By proclaiming the arrival of the kingdom of God, Jesus invited hearers to believe that his powerful and loving Father was working in and through him. His words and deeds were an invitation to accept the salvation promised by the Jewish prophets.

Stage 2. After the resurrection of Jesus, his chosen followers continued the mission entrusted to them. They preached, taught as Jesus did, baptized, and incorporated others into the new covenant community (Matt 28:18-20). During the extended period of oral catechesis, apostolic preachers developed standard patterns (called *Formen* in German) to portray various aspects of the ministry of Jesus.

The specific features of these oral patterns were determined by a variety of circumstances, such as liturgical usage, audience interest, apologetics, controversies, and the need for practical guidance for new converts. As a result, these oral patterns became more than simple repetitions of what the earthly Jesus said and did. They also incorporated the postresurrection faith of early Christian believers. This faith dimension was decisive in shaping both content and form of Christian preaching, that is, what was remembered and how it was expressed.

Stage 3. The actual composition of the Synoptic Gospels was the final stage of this long development. The evangelists creatively selected from many oral traditions and from primitive written accounts of the words and deeds of Jesus. They molded these into the unified narratives that paint a picture of his ministry, suffering, and glorification, which continue to have impact and appeal.

This third stage of the formation of the Gospels occurred toward the end of the apostolic age (65-95 C.E.), the period when original eyewitnesses of the earthly Jesus were rapidly disappearing. This marks the final stage of the "Christ event," the privileged period of God's revelation in his incarnate Son. The success of the Gospels of Mark, Matthew, and Luke effectively eliminated the earlier accounts about Jesus mentioned in Luke 1:1. Those shorter writings were no longer copied. They are not part of the "canon" of the New Testament, the official list of normative Christian Scripture.

Obviously many remnants of these primitive accounts have been incorporated into the three Synoptic Gospels. This is the major reason why the three are so similar. The complex problem of the literary relationship between Matthew, Mark, and Luke is known as "the Synoptic problem," a technical question that will not be studied in this book. The Gospels do not allow us to know everything about Jesus. But they enable us to do something more important, to know Jesus.

I used the term "evangelist" to designate the authors of the Gospels. The word is related to the Greek term meaning "good news." It is found in the New Testament only three times and always refers to preachers. Only later did "evangelist" become the technical term for the writers of the four Gospels. None of the authors uses the word as a term of self-designation. In fact, all the Gospels were published anonymously.

The mention of authors is a reminder that the Gospels were composed not only as faith documents but also as literary creations. As literary texts they both mirror life and create a world. They are God's saving word but also words of human authors. As creations of true literary authors, the Gospels require an audience that responds to their faith thrust and enters into their artistic world. Like other religious masterpieces, they survive because of their profound impact and ongoing appeal. The subject matter, the fidelity of Jesus in laying down his life as "ransom" for humans, has unique import for believing readers (see Mark 10:45; Matt 20:28).

Preparing to Study the Four Gospels

To enter into the story of Jesus as narrated in the Gospels, a reader needs to become familiar with each one of them as a structured story. Each Gospel is a distinct literary whole, designated to teach and to touch. To experience their religious power demands an imaginative reading and rereading of each as a faith document evoking personal response. Their imaginative impact invites modern readers to become familiar with their social background, which explains many persons, objects, and events of the story.

This introduction seeks to build on reader interest and to foster individual reflection on and dialogue with the Christ event. Its special feature is to apply contemporary insights into how language communicates to these foundational writings of apostolic Christian tradition. This approach rejects the sharp distinction some commentators make between oral and written cultures. They see a sharp break or even a change of purpose between the oral preaching of the good news and the written Gospels. My study of the background, content, and development of the Synoptics does not reveal them as reactions against oral apostolic tradition.

Writing was necessary to preserve the memory of significant events of the mission of Jesus for a universal audience in future generations. The shift from listening to reading is one that had become common hundreds of years before the time of Jesus and the ministry of his disciples. Written documents had formed part of Jewish worship and teaching for centuries. These Scriptures were cited by Jesus himself and were invoked as witness to Jesus by early Christian preachers.

The transition to the stage of written Gospels did not cause a shift in the nature of the Christian Church as the worshiping community that loved the Lord Jesus too much to let his memory die. Quite the contrary. The Gospels were the Church's response to special needs created by the death of the apostles and eyewitnesses of Jesus, as will be explained in the next chapter.

Concrete details about the process by which the evangelists, whom tradition calls Matthew, Mark, Luke, and John, brought the Gospels into existence cannot be traced with certainty by modern biblical scholars. No documents are available to provide such information as, Who were their authors? Where were they composed? When were they first published? To what particular group or community was each one addressed?

Modern historical and critical biblical studies have developed a whole range of critical disciplines to examine the sources and growth of the Gospels. Once a believer has become familiar with the documents themselves, these methods can be helpful and enlightening for appreciating the message. I will treat them briefly in the next chapter. As a whole, however, this study guide does not focus on such "diachronic" questions, that is, on stages during the oral period that led to the composition of the Synoptics and of John.

My focus is "synchronic," that is, it examines the four Gospels in their final form as complete literary entities about the earthly life of Jesus as Messiah. In keeping with the nature of religious writing at that time, the Gospels were not "original" compositions in the modern sense of flowing from the creative imagination of their authors. Their aim was just the opposite. Their goal was to preserve intact the apostolic Church's memory of the incarnate Lord, who revealed God's plan of salvation under the guidance of the Holy Spirit.

The early Church's memory of Jesus was complex, and it varied according to the communities in which it was celebrated. Each of these individual memories had its own integrity and beauty and produced a distinctive presentation. To illustrate this, I devote a separate chapter to each of the Gospels: to Mark in chapter 4, to Matthew in chapter 5, to Luke in chapter 7, and to John in chapter 11.

Fidelity to the community's faith commitment directed the care with which each of these narratives was preserved and finally "canonized," that is, accepted by the Church among its official Scripture as the writings that form the basis of its belief and activity. In other words, the Gospels are "normative" for Christian faith. I explain the term "normative" now and will illustrate its functioning in the chapter on parables (ch. 6), on miracles (ch. 8), on the passion of Jesus (ch. 9), and on the resurrection (ch. 10).

The Gospels as Normative Writings

By the end of the second century of the Christian era, the four Gospels were accepted by Christian communities throughout the world as filled with the spirit of the apostles and as appropriate for reading in the celebration of the Eucharist. They were judged capable of communicating the one apostolic faith by their fidelity to the primitive tradition.

These writings, growing out of apostolic wisdom and truth, as the Dogmatic Constitution on Divine Revelation of Vatican II teaches, stand above the Church. It needs to listen to them and to mold its belief and life-style according to their teaching. The Synoptic Gospels are rooted in the faith of eyewitnesses of the earthly Jesus and call readers to grow in that same faith. Consequently, they come under the heading of "revelation" in the theological sense of a self-manifestation of God's mysterious plan of salvation.

The Letter to the Ephesians calls revelation "the plan of God's favor" (3:2). The Greek Fathers of the Church refer to revelation as "the economy," the way God manages the household of creation to bring Jews and Gentiles into one new people "in the blood of Christ," that is, through his redemptive death (Eph 3:13).

The Gospel narratives are thus the norms by which believers live. They are meant to be read as an urgent appeal to become "one new creature," the living community of Christ reconciled "in one body to God through the cross" (Eph 2:15-17). The challenge of the Gospels to the Church in every age is to bring to bear on society the power of Christ's redemption by living according to his model in love and hope, in unity and service.

As Pope Paul VI explained to teachers of Scripture, those who interpret the Bible must fulfill a double fidelity. They must be faithful (1) to the biblical text as it has come down in tradition by explaining its meaning in its original cultural and sociolinguistic setting and (2) to their contemporary believers by elucidating the message of Scripture in language and imagery that invite the present generation to experience the impact and appeal of the Gospels (*Osservatore Romano*, English Edition, October 8, 1970).

The following chapters develop a method of reading the Gospels that respects their nature as literary documents and incorporates achievements of contemporary language and historical research.

FOLLOW UP

A rapid reading of the three Synoptic Gospels along with these introductory chapters is an important element in the process of developing a personal method of studying them as normative writings of Christian Scriptures. As you read them, let them raise questions for your further study and discussion. Let them stimulate the dialogue of faith as you move to a deeper understanding of each Gospel.

At the same time, it is good to check on your "cultural literacy" about New Testament times. If you are unfamiliar with the terminology and institutions of the Greco-Roman world of the time of Jesus, now is the time to become acquainted with terms that appear in the New Testament, such as Pharisees, Sadducees, Passover, covenant, mysteries. A reliable guide is Sean Freyne, *The World of the New Testament* (Wilmington, Del.: Michael Glazier, 1980).

2

A Method for Gospel Study

The Gospels have always formed the core for Christian praying, preaching, and exhortation. Many Fathers of the Church composed homilies based on them, either on an entire Gospel or on some particular part, like the passion or the Sermon on the Mount. The homiletic method of an ancient preacher familiar with rhetoric (like St. John Chrysostom) would be to explain the text carefully and then to make moral applications. He would often cite other parts of the Bible to bolster his argument.

The learned African Father of the Church St. Augustine wrote a long treatise entitled *On the Agreement of the Books of the Four Evangelists*. His aim was to demonstrate that all the Gospels, despite their differences, proclaimed the same truths about Jesus. All of these early commentators accepted the Gospels as inspired by the Holy Spirit and as setting norms for the Church's faith and practice. They studied and preached the Gospels for their spiritual insights and moral guidance (see 2 Tim 3:16).

These homilies of the Fathers of the Church still offer believers helpful and challenging insights into the Gospels. Their method of studying the Gospels continued in a systematic and academic form during the Middle Ages under the influence of the Scholastic theologians, who composed commentaries on many of the writings of the Old and New Testaments.

After the Age of Enlightenment of the eighteenth century, the Gospels became a subject of religious controversy. Concern for the historicity of the earthly Jesus increased apologetic interest in the Catholic Church to affirm the truth of the Gospels. The Church reacted negatively to the historical-critical method, the prevailing approach in academic study of the Gospels, which began before the end of the nineteenth century.

Historical criticism is a diachronic method of study, that is, it focuses attention on the process by which the Gospels came into being. It emphasizes the forces and motives that influenced their authors: why they wrote, the sources they used, the community situations to which they reacted. This scholarly approach recognizes that the Gospels went through a long period of oral development between the death of Jesus about 30 C.E. and the final creative editing of the texts of Matthew, Mark, and Luke during the second half of the first century.

Historical criticism is an empirical approach that incorporates a variety of methods. Critical students of the Gospel differ in the way they employ the variety of approaches available. In a simplified way, the four most common kinds of historical criticism now employed by scholars of the Gospels are as follows:

Form Criticism studies how the smallest literary "forms" or units developed to proclaim the words and deeds of Jesus originated within the early Church or apostolic community. These small units included short narratives of controversy, settings for sayings of Jesus, stories of healings, exorcisms, and other pieces about Jesus. They were created and formulated during the long oral period that preceded composition of the canonical Gospels.

Form criticism explains how primitive Christian preachers shaped the words and deeds of Jesus into such literary units as controversies with Jewish authorities, the ripostes of Jesus to difficult questions, scenes that showed him exercising the power of the kingdom of God. From traditions about the ministry of Jesus the early Church distilled brief summaries of parables and began to organize oral material into collections of narratives and teachings.

Source Criticism investigates the earliest stages of the complex variety of topics preserved in the Gospels to determine where they came from. Did the evangelists use oral or written sources? Did they modify these sources? What forces were at work to influence composition? The purpose of source criticism is to determine what elements were incorporated into the final text of the Gospels and what influences they represent.

Historical Criticism is a reflective form of the critical method that seeks to get behind the text and determine how many of the events narrated really happened in the earthly life of Jesus, how the texts that were handed down relate to original events, and how much of the discourse is his actual teaching. It reflects the modern desire to know what really happened.

Redaction Criticism is the branch of the critical method that examines the personal contribution of the individual evangelists in shaping the final Gospel text. It seeks to uncover their theological suppositions and other motives that influenced the way they put the Gospels together.

For a long period the Catholic Church took a negative view of historical criticism, seeing such critical methods as manifestations of skepticism toward the revelation of the earthly Jesus. The use of historical criticism was judged to be the fruit of ideologies hostile to divine intervention in the world and to belief in the divine inspiration of Scripture. However, as historical methodology became more reliable, the Catholic Church's Biblical Commission endorsed critical method in its instruction "On the Historical Truth of the Gospels," issued on April 21, 1964. This instruction paved the way for the Church's acceptance of biblical criticism in the Dogmatic Constitution on Divine Revelation of Vatican II, issued on November 18, 1965.

Students of the Gospel need to remember that historical-critical methodology is scientific rather than theological. As such, it does not deal with the Gospels in terms of their original religious purpose, namely, to nourish the faith of members of believing communities. It cannot offer the final judgment on their religious meaning as literary products of faith. A theological method that draws upon the nature of Gospels as canonical or normative is still needed to enable believers to draw from the inspired wisdom of these artistic compositions displaying unity, coherence, and prominence. For this reason the historical-critical method does not form the basis of this introduction to the Gospels.

Approach of This Book

Believers accept the four Gospels as the Word of God. Yet they are also human words. As products of human authors, they require the same kind of competence on the part of their readers as any other artistic text. Each Gospel has its own special appeal, which seeks to evoke a favorable response from readers who approach it with an openness to its impact and message. That need provides the direction for this introduction. It focuses on the rhetorical power of language employed by the evangelists to communicate the message of Jesus as sign of God's wisdom, compassion, and saving gifts for all humanity.

The Synoptics employ the primary religious language of primitive Christian tradition to communicate the divine revelation of Jesus and his earthly companions. The vehicle chosen by the evangelists to portray the mission of Jesus was narrative, or story. This choice has a whole series of implications for readers, because the form draws them into the story of God's active involvement in human salvation through the words and deeds of his chosen Messiah, Jesus. The evangelists involve and shape the lives of readers by the way they organized the plot of their accounts of that mission: what they omit, what they emphasize, how they arrange the scenes to create impact and appeal. All of this takes place within the shaping principle of the literary genre of gospel, which will be explained in the next chapter.

As narratives, then, the Synoptic Gospels share two qualities of story as a literary form:

1. Like every story, the Synoptics leave gaps, either because the authors did not know about certain events or because they judged that some incidents did not contribute to the story as they wished to tell it. Readers must be competent to recognize the hints of the evangelists about what is important in plot development and learn how to analyze the characters. Above all, readers must identify with Jesus as he carries out his divine mission. He does so by responding totally to God's guiding Spirit, even to the surrender of his life as ransom for human beings.

After his profound religious experience on the occasion of his baptism by John and his initiation into his role as proclaimer of the kingdom of God, Jesus displays his obedience to the Spirit by going into a deserted place to fast and pray for forty days, a symbolic time consecrated by events in the history of Israel. Throughout his mission Jesus becomes an exemplary symbol of fidelity for all believers. An essential part of reading the Gospels as story is a willingness to be formed into the image of Jesus as it unfolds in relating to persons and events he encounters as God's Messiah.

Jesus is sign of God's saving presence to humanity. Readers want to understand how he relates to God, to the Spirit, to demons, to his family, to his disciples, to his enemies. As to the events narrated, readers ask how Jesus offers healing to the sick and to those possessed by demons. How does he confront ignorance, malice, deceit? How does he remain loyal to God in the face of plots against him and even betrayal by his own disciple?

The activities of all characters in the Gospels also perform as exemplary symbols, that is, they act as signs directing believers to renew their fidelity to the God of Jesus. So readers gain new insights into faith by identifying with other characters in the Gospels and by reflecting on their decisions and experiences.

2. Like every story, the Gospels point beyond the immediate event. They invite readers to see these events as signs that shed light upon their role in the ongoing struggle between the kingdom of God and the forces of Satan, the adversary. Readers cannot sidestep decision but must choose between loyalty to the God of Jesus or be reckoned among the followers of Satan. Underlying their narrative is God's revelation, evoking in readers obedience to the call that Jesus gives to take up the cross and follow him.

Participation of Readers

It is clear, then, that a fruitful reading of the four Gospels demands active participation by readers who involve themselves as committed believers. The insights of sociolinguists on text reception and of "reader response criticism" provide helpful techniques to foster this personal engagement. For the text of each Gospel is a complex process that creates a symbolic universe that invites committed dialogue partners to enter. The chapters in this book that are devoted to each of the individual Gospels will point out ways to show how the rhetoric of each invites readers to respond to its personal presentation of Jesus as God's Messiah.

If it is to be faithful to the traditional name "good news," each Gospel must become an inviting sign of salvation. Each of these religious creations is capable of addressing a variety of situations that confront believers today: issues of social justice; the challenges of peace; the various forms of political and economic oppression and exploitation rampant today, as well as the environmental issues that cry out for solutions.

Believers in today's complex society have to make special efforts to find a connection between the story of Jesus narrated in the Gospels and its abiding religious applications as well as applications to the modern world. To do so they must be competent to capture the power of the original revelation experience as embodied in the primary religious language of the four Gospels. These texts often come across as dull in a rapid reading because "we have heard it all before." They have been repeated so often and commented upon in abstract or technical language that does not speak to the contemporary idiom.

A fruitful method for hearing the revolutionary message of the Gospels in their original power must challenge modern readers to wrestle with the texts. Readers need to learn how to reflect on the narratives on a variety of levels by using available resources of literary criticism, the modern term for the ancient discipline of rhetoric.

Since the entire Gospel as a literary whole is both context and tool for understanding, the approach to studying the Gospels proceeds on two levels:

1. On the level of macrostructure, that is, viewing each Gospel as a unified literary creation. Each Gospel moves with dramatic swiftness from the call of Jesus to his unselfish display of fidelity to God on Calvary. Then, suddenly, the Father, who seemed to abandon Jesus to his opponents, dramatically intervenes to exalt Jesus and justify his mission in the resurrection narratives. The elements of this macrostructure will be explained in the next chapter.

2. On the level of microstructure, that is, looking at the individual parts and literary figures of each Gospel. It is at the level

of individual episodes and discourses that the resources of rhetoric can be fruitfully employed to achieve an appreciation of the organic power of the Gospels to enable readers to feel communion with Jesus in all aspects of his saving mission. Then readers can identify with the experience of Jesus.

The rest of this chapter will describe the two elements of microstructure that give the Gospels their impact and appeal, namely, the nature of religious language and the factors and functions of the speech act. A look at these elements show that the Gospels were written not so much to give readers information about the past Jesus as to portray the spiritual power that his presence was still evoking in the believing community.

Religious Language. This is a code term for the dimension of communication that links readers to the transcendent and directs them toward God's demands. It is an appeal for personal commitment to the revelation of Jesus. The aim of the Gospels is to communicate "the mind of Christ," to arouse readers to activate the habit of faith that is dead unless it remains operative in love.

The common sharing of the four Gospels in the faith setting of Christian community is capable of releasing the power of the redemption as the healing force in human relations. The imaginative interaction between readers and the values displayed by Jesus in healing the sick, encouraging the weak, preaching the good news to the poor, and offering his life as ransom for humanity generates the type of religious responsibility that transforms the Church and makes it a sign of God's redemptive humanity in the world.

The Gospels call each age to dialogue anew with the roots of Christian faith and to develop new styles of commitment to the value changes needed for world peace and justice. Because gospel imagery is so rich, with an excess of meaning and power, it is capable of being translated into other literary, artistic, and sacramental forms that support this same response.

Factors and Functions of Speech Acts. Religious language is bound by the rules governing all linguistic communication. As pieces of religious communication, the Gospels contain the language factors humans employ in mutual interaction. After years of studying how language operates, the great linguist Roman Jakobson reduced the factors of a speech act to six: a *sender*, by establishing physical and psychological *contact*, sends a spoken or written *message* in a specific *context* by using a mutually known *code* to *receptors*, whether listeners or readers.

These six factors operate in the Gospels. The evangelists used them to make the good news available to believers of any time or place. Because of great differences between the social and cultural situations that separate Jesus from modern readers, they must have some awareness of transcultural anthropology to grasp the fullness of the gospel message today.

This flexibility and adaptability of language to new cultural situations led Roman Jakobson to postulate six functions of the speech act in addition to the six factors. These functions vary according to the situation of the communication event. Briefly, the *emotive* function determines the *poetic* features of the *referential* import of the message. The *evocative* force it generates within receptors relies on the figures of speech, which serve the *phatic* function of keeping receptors alert. In case the communication breaks down, the sender draws upon the *metalinguistic* function to clarify the message.

By becoming more aware of these factors and functions, readers of the Gospels can better experience their impact and appeal. The evangelists not only shared intellectual insights about the teaching of Jesus but also evoked emotional attachments for him as well as admiration and wonder at his activities. The Gospels draw upon the aesthetic resources of language to inform the minds and transform the lives of readers with the aim of evoking new commitments among believers. The chapters devoted to the Gospels of Matthew, Mark, Luke, and John will illustrate how gospel language operates on a microlevel in individual passages. The commentary will illustrate why they still appeal to believers.

The burden of this book is that modern readers need special guidance to hear the Gospels in a society that has great cultural differences from that in which Jesus lived.

FOLLOW UP

The best response for readers who wish to enter more fully into the Synoptic Gospels at this point is to continue to read them as stories. That is the way to become familiar with each one as a whole and with the characters and events found in them. Each one has its own thrust and character, which will be treated in later chapters.

As you study the next chapter on the shaping principle of the gospel genre, raise questions as to why these relatively short narratives continue to arouse hearts to discipleship. Additional material on the approach followed in this book is found in William A. Beardslee, *Literary Criticism of the New Testament* (Philadelphia: Fortress, 1970).

3

The Shape of a Gospel

Chapter 1 explained the composition of the four Gospels within the social context of the early Christian communities as the third stage of the unfolding of the story of Jesus. The first stage was the earthly ministry of Jesus. The second was the initial period of the Church's preaching and reflection, of establishing worshiping communities throughout the existing Roman Empire. It was a time of oral instruction to educate new believers in the Christian movement.

With respect to the third stage of the Church's growth, the actual composition of written gospels, this chapter addresses two questions: Why did these faith documents of the newly formed Christian movement take the literary form that was later given the name "gospel"? What constitutes or shapes a gospel? In other words, what are the essential elements needed to create this new literary form? Readers should know these features of those early Christian writings, which enabled the new community of faith to survive after the death of the immediate companions of Jesus and even to thrive amid the great social and cultural changes taking place.

Why Gospels Are Necessary

The death of the first generation of Christians created a crisis for the survival of the movement. Jesus had announced that he was proclaiming the arrival of the kingdom of God, that is, God's intervening to rule the world. In reality, however, his activities brought about no significant changes in the prevailing social and political institutions. Instead, by the end of their lives his followers had merely set up a number of small worshiping communities throughout the Roman Empire. In the public sphere these communities were gradually seen as distinct from the official Judaism to which Jesus belonged.

These followers of Jesus claimed to enjoy the gifts of the Holy Spirit, poured into their hearts by the risen Lord. They went forth gathering others into their communities of mutual love and transcendent faith.

What was the link between these scattered groups and the kingdom of God that Jesus had proclaimed? What world-changing events were happening in them as they came together to celebrate the death of the Lord in their Eucharistic meal? Some of their members started to compose short pieces about the activities of the earthly Jesus. They recalled his controversial stances, like eating with sinners and saying that God wanted Sabbath observances to serve human needs (see Luke 13). They put some of his provocative parables into writing and told stories about his driving demons out of the sick. They claimed that the parables illustrated how the kingdom of God had truly arrived in and with Jesus (see Matt 13).

Written descriptions of the brilliant responses of Jesus to opponents challenging his teaching circulated. Through these writings of Christian apostles and prophets, Jesus became a dialogue partner to followers who had never seen him. Yet these short pieces did not have the necessary breadth of vision to keep the memory of Jesus alive in a way that would build the symbolic universe needed to sustain the faith of future generations of believers.

Thanks to the missionary activity of eyewitnesses, the Christian movement was able to survive and grow for a whole generation. Their faith and courageous witness made available the message of salvation promised by God through Jesus Christ without any written texts. The infant Church could witness because it possessed three unique gifts: (1) the cultic celebrations of its faith, especially the Eucharistic memorial of the Lord's death and resurrection; (2) the practice of unselfish love, whether in life or in death, in imitation of Jesus; and (3) Christ's message of saving truth. How does the creation of gospel as a literary form relate to these three unique gifts of the Church?

1. As long as the original eyewitnesses were still present within the community to respond to questions about the words and work of Jesus, they provided a stabilizing and satisfying teaching authority. Their living voice sustained the other two gifts, love and communal worship, bequeathed to his followers by the earthly Jesus. These apostolic witnesses could remind believers that they were able to enter into the transcendent praise offered to God by the risen Lord Jesus because they were incorporated into the body of Christ through baptism.

In sharing in the Eucharist meal, believers recall and make present his unique act of worship as a bond of faith until Jesus shall return in glory. The bonding with Christ achieved by initiation into his body by faith and baptism continues to provide strength and motivation for believers to conduct themselves as he did (1 Cor 6:13-20). Participation in the sacrament of the Eucharist is sharing in the new covenant sacrifice of Christ's self-offering. Consequently, to enter into that act of worship with malice is to share in the guilt of putting Jesus to death (1 Cor 11:23-27).

At the Last Supper, Jesus did not merely enable but ordered his followers to remember that sacramental act. It was the most important sign of his coming death as ransom for the salvation of fallen humanity. Obedient to his command, Christians developed the cultic expressions that were to mark their identification with the worship Jesus offered to the Father in accomplishing his saving mission. Nothing in these rites makes them dependent upon time or place or particular persons. Hence, even after the death of the eyewitnesses, they continue to nourish believers of every age to be faithful members of Christ's body.

2. The same continuity exists in the case of the second gift that shapes the nature of the Christian community, namely, unselfish love after the example of Jesus. This love extends beyond the immediate disciples of Jesus. The plea of Jesus, "Love one another as I have loved you" (John 13:34), continues to challenge his followers in every time and place and station of life. Jesus sets himself up as model for that kind of life by his personal conduct at

every moment, but above all by his limitless love in his courageous and obedient death. He excludes no one from his forgiveness. As the seed that dies to give life (see John 12:24), Jesus
empowers believers to mature in love.

3. But apostolic faith and teaching witness created a real problem. A speech act requires continuity, physical and psychological, between sender and receiver of the message. Only those
contemporaries of Jesus who actually experienced him as a human
being, who heard his preaching and teaching, who were touched
by intimate contact with him, could call themselves authentic in-
terpreters of his revelation.

The eyewitnesses had a double basis for their witness. They
knew Jesus first as a man filled with a holy spirit. His life showed
that he was chosen by God, and they opened themselves to his
unique revelation. Further, they were also shaped and instructed
by the mystery of his resurrection and the reception to the Holy
Spirit. This heavenly power enabled them to come to the fullness
of understanding about Jesus and his unique place in God's saving plan. As long as they were active in evangelizing, they could
nourish the Church's faith. Their witness contained the primary
religious language of personal experience.

But these apostolic witnesses were human. They were subject
to persecution, the limitations of old age, and death. How were
they to make their apostolic faith and knowledge about Jesus
available to Christians of future ages?

To provide the gift of apostolic teaching about Jesus in a personal way explains the existence of the Gospels. Christian faith
in the role of the Holy Spirit in continuing the saving presence
of Jesus in history is crucial for understanding how the Synoptic
Gospels function. The powerful presence of the Holy Spirit is the
ground of Christian belief in the divine inspiration of the Holy
Scriptures. The Spirit prompted and empowered certain members
of the apostolic community to create a new literary form that
would embody and transmit its unique faith in Jesus to future
believers.

This new model of writing originally had no special name. Only
later was the name "gospel" assigned to it on the basis of its content, the good news of salvation. Its original formulation is usually
attributed by historical critics to Mark, and the extant Gospel of

Mark is hailed as a triumph of his personal literary genius. That writing, as well as the three other Gospels included in the New Testament, encompasses the essentials of apostolic faith in Jesus. All four continue to guide Christian communities and to insure that apostolic authority remains a stabilizing element of the one, holy, catholic, and apostolic Church.

The Shaping Principle of Gospel

The essential and determining elements of this new literary form, "gospel," a unique type of writing, are five:

1. Jesus is introduced as the divinely chosen Messiah. He comes to proclaim the arrival of a new saving presence of God, which he calls the kingdom of God. The choice of Jesus for this mission is linked to his asking to receive the baptism of John the Baptizer. John hesitates because he anticipates a purifying judgment of God upon Israel, but Jesus acts because he senses that many promises made by the Lord through Israel's chosen prophets are coming to fulfillment in him.

2. Jesus is immediately tested as God's Son to verify that he is faithful to his call and ready to submit his mission to the direction of God's Spirit. This testing takes place in the wilderness as a battleground between God and Satan. The forty-day test is presented in stark brevity by Mark but is elaborated in a graphic narrative of three temptations by Matthew and Luke (Mark 1:13; Matt 4:1-11; Luke 4:1-13).

3. Jesus goes forth from his victory over Satan to reveal the presence of the kingdom of God in word and deed, especially by striking parables and mighty deeds of healing. The bulk of all four Gospels is made up of narratives describing how Jesus carries out his mission. First, he gathers and forms disciples. Then he leads the life of a wandering preacher in a way that gives witness to the power of the kingdom of God at work in his own life.

The literary nature of his parables as narrative metaphors also conveys insights into that kingdom and the response it demands from humans. His ability to exorcise demons displays his power as God's Son over the reign of evil in the world.

In the Gospels, both parables and miracles are revelations, that is, their primary goal is not to instruct about events within the grasp of human knowledge. Rather, parables and miracles proclaim that in Jesus God is making a new, abundant outpouring of divine power available to humans, a loving favor that frees them from slavery to the forces of evil. That is what the kingdom of God is about. These two forms of revelation will be treated in detail: parables in chapter 6 and miracles in chapter 8.

This revelation of God's activity by Jesus first meets with enthusiasm and a certain degree of acceptance by the common people of Galilee. Those who benefit by his healing power follow him as the one they hope will restore Israel's long-lost political independence. They long for freedom from political tyranny and Roman oppression and envision Jesus as a royal messianic liberator.

4. Jesus rejects this response to his proclamation of the kingdom of God. When he makes this clear, his success turns sour and his preaching meets with resistance. The kingdom of God that he reveals differs from the projections of Jewish leaders of his day. They come to see Jesus as a rival. He is a threat to their control of the Temple of Jerusalem and the cult centered around it.

Jewish priests are threatened by the attitude of Jesus toward the Mosaic Torah, the instructions that govern their religious life. With the help of one of the closest disciples of Jesus, the religious authorities of Israel join forces with the occupying Roman powers and arrest him. They have him tried, convicted as a blasphemer, and put to death as a rival to Roman civil authority. On the human level this death would have marked the end of the Jesus movement.

5. The shaping principle of gospel, however, contains a further element, namely, divine vindication of Jesus and his mission. Jesus, faithful to his own directive, "Do not resist evil" (Matt 5:39), goes to his death in obedience to his Father's will. He believes that the cross is an expression of God's plan to reconcile humanity to himself, not to reject them. By raising Jesus from among the dead, the Father vindicates this fidelity of Jesus and makes him mediator of the new covenant and Lord of the new age.

This one shaping principle organizes, unifies, and gives coherence to all four Gospels. Each evangelist presents the same story of Jesus in a personal way, creatively adapting to changing audiences and social conditions. Separate chapters will explain how this shaping principle functions in the Gospels of Matthew, Mark, Luke, and John. Each of them embodies the unique apostolic faith and thus preserves the normative witness to the Christ event.

At stated above, Christ's message of saving truth is the third unique gift that the early Church had to give to future generations. Christians keep returning to these inspired and authoritative documents for revealed guidance concerning the person and mission of Jesus. They illustrate why Vatican II affirms in its constitution on revelation that the Church does not stand above Scripture but listens to it and is shaped by it in apostolic faith and practice.

Because of the simplicity of this shaping principle of gospel, readers can easily imagine the structure and literary unity and religious impact of each one. By keeping the shaping principle in focus as they study individual scenes, they see where each narrative and discourse of Jesus fits into the whole. They begin to relate each part of the gospel to the entire mission of Jesus as it unfolds.

This method of studying the Gospels is fruitful for personal identification with Jesus because the work as a whole is both context and tool for understanding each part of a gospel. Knowing or experiencing a gospel means more than understanding single words and sentences. Through this holistic approach, readers see how the stories told about the mission of Jesus as events that reveal the kingdom of God relate to their own salvation and to the transformation of human values.

Gospels as Cult Proclamations

This understanding of the nature of gospel as a literary form created to serve the Christian Church points to its function within the community in every age. Gospels came into being primarily as aids to worship, as liturgical documents. They are cult proclamations that shape the faith and celebrate the hope of believers. They were not written for private reading but to guide public proclamation and celebration. As such, they fall into the pattern of "remembering" that Jesus speaks about at the Last Supper. Remembering is a religious response to God's saving interventions among the chosen people.

Put in another way, the Gospels fit into the ongoing saving plan of the Lord by recalling his revelations to persons like Abraham in the vision related in Genesis 15 and to Moses on Mount Sinai (Exod 24). These favored servants of the Lord commemorated their revelation by erecting some kind of memorial shrine. Pilgrims would come to these shrines, especially on the anniversary of the event, to celebrate that divine appearance, known as a "theophany." The leader of the celebration, usually a priest, recited how God had appeared and what he said and did for his people on that occasion. This recitation is known as a "cult proclamation," a sacred story that is handed down from generation to generation to nourish the people's faith.

This cult-proclamation tradition is the background of the transfiguration scene in the Synoptics. Peter exclaims that it is good to be present in that sacred place, and he urges the erection of three commemorative tents (see Mark 9:5).

It is not surprising that when the Son of God became incarnate and proclaimed the kingdom of God, this saving divine intervention was commemorated by a new form of cult proclamation, not just a short account but a whole book. The Gospels have always played a significant role in Christian Eucharistic celebrations to explain what takes place in the sacrament. They foster faith in the mystery of the cross and resurrection of Jesus being celebrated. They continue to make the risen Jesus in glory available as dialogue partner for believing worshipers. In all these ways the Gospels serve the performative function of fostering social transformation and ongoing conversion of the celebrating community.

Jesus is God's epiphany, not only for the few years of his earthly life but as Son of God once incarnate in human flesh and blood and now clothed in risen glory. His whole earthly life was and remains a powerful revelation of God's love. That life was lived under the direction of the Holy Spirit, who led Jesus to confront God's enemies with the intention of freeing humans from slavery to sin. Under the guidance of this Holy Spirit, that life of Jesus was translated into literary form to aid the healing of believers of all ages.

When read in this horizon of faith, the Gospels yield their full revelation. This revelatory function of the Gospels accounts for their brevity. They organize the words and mighty deeds of Jesus as God's way of communicating the saving power still available in and through him. They do not concern themselves with a variety of details that do not contribute to their goal, as much as we would like to know about them. This unique form of apostolic revelation also explains why the Gospels could originate only from believing witnesses linked in a concrete historical way to the apostolic community.

These writings are gifts from early believers to believers of every age. They remain a question mark to those who refuse to open their minds and hearts to the possibility of God's salvation in Jesus. Before our more detailed examination of the individual Gospels, this overview of their "shaping principle," their overarching unity and situation in God's saving plan, seeks to help readers follow the individual plot more fruitfully.

By keeping this shaping principle in mind, readers can recognize that each Gospel is composed as an organic embodiment of community tradition. This approach may sound strange to Christians who have encountered the Gospels only as short pieces read in a Sunday liturgy. Believers who seldom or never read a Gospel through in a single setting still need to become acquainted with this shaping principle and keep it in the back of their mind in reading individual passages. This overarching unity draws them into the divine plan of which they are part. They can see each Gospel as a narrative of the final act in God's self-revelation in history, as a description of the way he brings humans to repentance and new life in Jesus Christ. Each Gospel is a personal invitation to its reader to enter into God's saving activity by taking up the cross and following Jesus.

Evangelists as Authors

Only the three Synoptic Gospels and John were accepted by the Christian community as written under the inspiration of the Holy Spirit to guide the faith and practice of believers. Mark is primarily a stark yet vivid narrative, shaped to focus on Jesus as suffering Messiah, doomed to die as "ransom" for the sins of humanity (Mark 10:45). The bulk of Mark's material comes from tradition, from stories told about Jesus during the oral period when apostolic preachers guided believers by short accounts about Jesus. In this sense, Mark is not like a modern author whose aim is to be original and strikingly creative.

Despite his devotion to tradition, Mark is a real author who forms this traditional material into a new literary genre by bringing original theological and religious goals to bear on it. He even calls attention to his material at significant points. Thus, he notes that when Jesus says that it is not what enters the mouth but what comes out of the human heart that defiles, he is "purifying all foods" (Mark 7:19). And speaking of the frightening "abomination of desolation," he advises, "let the reader understand," namely, that the Temple will be desecrated (Mark 13:14). An analysis of the entire Gospel of Mark is the subject of chapter 4.

Matthew enriches the shaping principle of gospel by some personal contributions. First, he adds several major sermons of Jesus and places them strategically throughout the Gospel to provide content for Christian teachers. He also draws heavily upon the Jewish Scriptures to portray the entire public life of Jesus as their fulfillment. These changes illustrate that Matthew is a true author. His orderly and comprehensive approach make his Gospel a favorite text for Christian pastors and preachers of homilies. What Matthew does with the shaping principle of gospel will be treated in chapter 5.

Luke, who comes across strongly as a writer familiar with the needs of Greek-speaking non-Jewish believers, brings literary polish and ethical concerns to his version of the mission of Jesus. He keeps in mind that Gentile converts to the Christian movement living in the permissive society of the Roman Empire need to find in Jesus and his disciples models of wisdom and integrity. His story of Jesus encourages enthusiastic discipleship. The distinctive features of the Gospel of Luke will be studied in chapter 7. John goes his own way, as chapter 11 will show.

The literary form of gospel determines that all four evangelists transmit the primary religious experience of the apostolic encounter with Jesus in story form. They do not write as systematic theologians composing abstract treatises for believers. On the contrary, they recapture the fresh, exciting spiritual journey of original followers of Jesus. They stretch language beyond its ordinary limits to communicate the new vision of the Father, which Jesus enjoyed and shared. In other words, the four Gospels present the saving mission of Jesus in language that presses against the world of the transcendent, which Jesus called the kingdom, or rule, of God. These narratives enable readers to participate in the transforming reality of the Christ event.

Much of the terminology of the Gospels would later become fixed in Church tradition and provide the basis for dogmatic and moral tracts by systematic theologians. Christian believers, like humans dedicated to any cause, eventually organized their original religious experience into a belief system and translated it into abstract concepts that hardened the language of revelation.

By its very nature as witness literature, the literary form of gospel is transitional. It could remain available as a mode of expression only during the formative period of the Christian community. Then it was destined to be superseded by a variety of more systematic and catechetical and aesthetical writings that would address the apologetic and educational and ethical needs of Church members.

As cultural conditions change and Christians, like the rest of the world, become more secular, it becomes harder for them to uphold the demands of gospel values. The aim of the chapters devoted to the individual Gospels is to build a bridge that will enable modern Christians to appreciate and dialogue with these foundational writings of the Church. That is the first step for finding in them wellsprings of prayerful reflection and faith witness.

FOLLOW UP

The more readers develop their "cultural literacy" of the environment of Jesus and his disciples, the easier will it be to integrate the shaping principle of the gospel form into their study of the individual Gospels. A help in terms of knowing the background of Jesus is Martin McNamara, *Palestinian Judaism and the New Testament* (Wilmington, Del.: Michael Glazier, 1983).

More emphasis on theological questions underlies the synthesis of Gerald S. Sloyan, *Jesus in Focus: A Life in Its Setting* (Mystic, Conn.:

Twenty-Third Publications, 1983). For literary insights, a helpful tool is Amos N. Wilder, *Early Church Rhetoric: The Language of the Gospel* (Cambridge, Mass.: Harvard University Press, 1971).

4

Mark: The Narrative Gospel

It is time now to enter into the literary world created by the apostolic faith in Jesus. The horizons of this world were gradually fleshed out over an entire generation of oral preaching. Once the original eyewitnesses were no longer able to preach as itinerant missionaries, the Holy Spirit guided them to preserve their faith vision in integrated narrative presentations of the mission of Jesus, the Synoptic Gospels. Most New Testament commentators attribute the creation of the literary form gospel to a disciple and secretary of Peter named Mark (see 1 Pet 5:13). He organized Peter's preaching into the five-point shaping principle described in the previous chapter.

Mark's opening words include the term that later became the title for this new literary form. They announce the perspective out of which he writes, "Start of the good news [gospel] of Jesus Christ, Son of God." This unusual title demands some interpretation. First of all, Mark presents this writing as a "start." The events of the mission of Jesus on earth were only the beginning of the good news that is still going on in the lives of all who believe in Jesus Christ.

This title recalls the necessity of reading this story keeping in mind the two thrusts of any great literary creation, (1) with a grasp of its overarching impact and appeal as a literary whole, following the story as it moves and responding to what it offers for enlightening minds and changing behavior; and (2) by analyzing the individual passages to experience how they draw readers into the mission of Jesus as it unfolds in a variety of ways.

The gospel guides readers to ratify the choices made by its hero "Jesus Christ, Son of God" (1:1). This phrase identifies Jesus by two titles. First, he is the "Christ," the Greek term for "the Anointed One," equivalent to the Hebrew title of "Messiah." This title tells readers that there is more significance for them in what they will hear about Jesus than the people who were dealing with Jesus on earth recognized at that time.

The followers of Jesus come to a clear understanding of him as the Messiah only gradually, through many doubts, mistakes, and misunderstandings during his life and by Spirit-filled reflection after his death. This tension between the readers, who now know who Jesus is, and the characters in the Gospel, who misjudge him during his life, creates an ironic dimension to the story. One aspect of that irony is called the "messianic secret." Jesus often tells those whom he cures (1:44; 5:43; 7:36; 8:26) and the demons he drives out of people (1:34; 3:12) not to tell anyone about what God is doing by his activity.

Readers find it ironic that Jesus wants his mighty deeds kept secret when they seem to be well known. The messianic secret is Mark's way of saying that the people involved are jumping to false conclusions. The reason Jesus appeals to secrecy is linked to the unfolding of his identity as Messiah. Until Jesus' saving mission is completed and he has proved his total fidelity to God, the real nature of his messiahship cannot be known. These calls for secrecy in Mark's narrative remind readers of that truth. This is his way of keeping believers aware of the danger of reducing Jesus to a worker of miracles.

The second phrase of Mark's title that reveals the identity of Jesus to readers is "Son of God." It tells readers that the entire mission of Jesus is carried out in obedience to the unfolding of God's plan. This title inserts Jesus into the perspective of God's intimate involvement in the world as Creator of all and as Savior through grace. The good news, then, is a revelation of the grace of God at work through his Son.

This grace is often designated by the term "salvation history." It is seen in the call of Abram, whose name was changed to Abraham, the father of many. Salvation history continued through the activity of Moses and the prophets and sages of Israel. It will reach new heights in the Son of God.

Mark roots his Gospel in that ongoing divine activity in history by introducing quotations from the prophets (Isa 40:3 and Mic 3:1 in Mark 1:2-3). He does this to remind readers that the work of Jesus must be understood in the context of the saving activity of God among the chosen people. In keeping with this thrust, the mission of Jesus merits the designation of "good news" (gospel). Since that term best describes the story Mark is about to unfold in story form, "gospel" eventually became not only the title but the way the literary form itself is designated.

The Overarching Structure of Mark's Gospel

How does Mark organize the five elements of the shaping principle of the new literary form, gospel, that he creates? He does so by creating a story that moves swiftly to give a synthetic vision of the mission of Jesus. His narrative includes details that allow it to serve as guide for the life and growth of members of local Christian communities.

Mark begins his brief introduction by presenting John the Baptizer. He is dressed like an ancient prophet and lives according to the austere prophetic ideal of prayer and fasting (1:4-6).

Jesus appears on the scene with no warning to undergo baptism from John. During that ceremony Jesus has a transcendent religious experience and hears a divine voice from heaven that designates him as God's "beloved Son" (1:9-11). From that moment Jesus proceeds under the direction of God's Spirit, who drives him out into the desert for a period of forty days. In this no-man's-land he is tested by the "Satan," or adversary, and proves that he is a loyal Son of God (1:13).

Immediately Jesus begins his mission of announcing, "The kingdom of God is here. Repent and put your faith in the good news" (1:15). The final stage of salvation history has arrived with this revelation by and in Jesus. In calling humans to repentance and salvation through faith in Jesus, God leaves himself open to the possibility of being rejected.

This double edge of revelation—divine gift and human freedom—always remains prominent in Mark's Gospel. It shapes the unfolding of the surface structure, or story line, which portrays how Jesus is rejected by his own people before being vindicated by God in the resurrection. Mark develops this mode of telling the story to remind readers that they, too, are responsible for choosing to accept or reject Jesus by their lives. Mark does not center on the earthly Jesus "back there" but on the living Son of God, who is calling readers to discipleship now.

The Gospel of Mark uses the "pattern of threes" as a key organizing tool for narrating the activity of Jesus. These cycles, developing the same theme or lesson, are an effective device to involve readers in the good news. They imitate the revelation of Jesus, which also passes through three stages: (1) his early success in the territory of Galilee in the northern part of the Holy Land (1:14–8:30); (2) the period that concentrates upon the faithful remnant, the twelve disciples who are willing to follow Jesus to Jerusalem and there to confront the opposition (8:31–10:52); and (3) the final week in the life of Jesus, which brings him to his death and resurrection (11:1–16:8), to which the final normative or canonical edition adds a summary of the resurrection appearances from the other Gospels (16:9-20).

Stage One: Revelation of Jesus as Messiah (1:14–8:30)

This part of Mark's Gospel illustrates the third item of the shaping principle of gospel, that is, revelation of the kingdom or rule of God by word and deed. Mark directs readers to draw a parallel between the demands the earthly Jesus makes on his hearers and the responsibility the risen Christ establishes for the believing community. He focuses on the relation between Jesus and his disciples by composing three cycles of revelation, each beginning with a short summary of the ministry of Jesus: Mark 1:14–3:6; 3:7–6:6a; 6:6b–8:30.

The technique of addressing the revelation to the disciples and the portrayal of their all-too-human responses provide readers with opportunities to identify with the earthly disciples of Jesus. In both a positive and negative way readers also respond to the good news that the glorious Lord Jesus continues to offer. The scenes as painted by Mark contrast the devotion of Jesus to those in need of salvation and the resistance Jesus experiences even from his chosen disciples.

These three cycles of revelation are designed in similar fashion, each one being made up of four parts: (1) an opening summary that places the events within the ministry of Jesus; (2) a scene that focuses on the disciples; (3) a longer sequence, during which Jesus carries out his role as Messiah by revealing how God is present in his preaching and mighty deeds; and (4) an act of misunderstanding or rejection on the part of recipients of this revelation. These smaller rejections anticipate and foreshadow the final rejection of Jesus by his people in Jerusalem.

The First Cycle of Revelation (1:14–3:6)

Summary. Mark gives a brief summary of the early ministry of Jesus in Galilee (1:14-15). He proclaims the good news that God's rule is now in place. The people need to repent and to adopt a life of trust.

Scene Involving Disciples (1:16-20). Without warning and with no elaboration of how this rule of God is going to be manifested, Jesus goes to the busy shore of the Lake of Galilee and abruptly calls two sets of brothers to follow him. They are fishers. He promises to make them "fishers of human beings."

Revelation in Word (1:21-45) *and Deed* (2:1–3:5). In schematic fashion Jesus goes about "teaching," in the Markan sense of illustrating how the kingdom of God is establishing a presence through his actions. Mark gives very little of the content of Jesus' teaching. Rather, he characterizes the success of Jesus in healing the sick and driving out demons as teaching "with authority" (1:22, 27). In fact, Jesus is so successful that he cannot even appear in towns lest he be overwhelmed by the crowds (1:45).

Rejection of Jesus (3:6). Response to the cures, the forgiving of sins, and the affirming that "the Son of Man is Lord even of the Sabbath" is swift in coming from a coalition of Pharisees and Herodians (2:28). They band together so that they might "do away with him." This marks the first foreshadowing of Jesus' rejection by his own people, a situation Mark emphasizes as a way of warning his audience not to be self-sufficient and faithless.

The Second Cycle of Revelation (3:7–6:6a)

Summary (3:7-12). Jesus expands his teaching activities beyond Galilee, even beyond the territory of the Jews, by going into the region of Tyre and Sidon.

The Appointment of the Twelve (3:13-19). Only Mark states that Jesus' reason for choosing the Twelve was "that they might be with him and that he might send them forth to proclaim" (3:14). This group enjoys deep interpersonal experience of Jesus.

Revelation in Word (3:20–4:34) *and Deed* (4:35–5:43). This section includes one of the two extended discourses of Jesus in the Gospel of Mark, the parable sermon (4:1-34). No additional narrative parable appears in Mark until chapter 12. Because parables are the distinctive method Jesus uses to reveal, they will be treated in detail in chapter 6.

Rejection (6:1-6a). After a period of successful teaching and healing, Jesus returns to his hometown, only to become a stumbling block for those who had thought they knew all about him. Their refusal to put faith in his mission causes him to be amazed and prevents miraculous activity on their behalf.

Third Cycle of Revelation (6:6b–8:30)

A Brief Summary (6:6b). This occupies only a single clause describing the activity of Jesus: "And he went through the villages in the vicinity teaching."

Scene with the Disciples (6:7-13, 30-32). Jesus sends the Twelve on a mission of healing and preaching repentance.

To create a sense of the passage of time for this preaching project, Mark inserts the story of the fate of John the Baptizer at the hands of Herod (6:14-29). When the Twelve return, they are called "apostles," the only time Mark uses the title by which they are best known in Christian tradition (6:30). They have experienced not only the exaltation of healing but also the strain of being overwhelmed by people desperately seeking cures. So Jesus arranges to take them away for needed rest.

Revelation in Word and Deed (6:33–8:26). This is a long and complicated development, in fact, a parallel development. It includes two accounts of Jesus' multiplying loaves and fishes for the crowds that follow him into deserted places (6:33-44; 8:1-9). Most commentators look upon these two narratives as two traditional versions of the same incident, one by Jewish Christians and the other by Gentile Christians. The event plays an extremely important part in preparing the apostles for the Eucharist meal at the Last Supper.

Another important revelation in this section of Mark arises out of criticism by "the Pharisees and some of their scribes" that Jesus and his disciples failed to observe Jewish ritual purifications (7:1-23). Jesus responds by accusing them of exalting human customs above God's commands. Then he gives an instruction on what alone can defile humans, namely, only what comes out of their heart. By declaring that food does not defile, Jesus (says Mark in an aside to his readers) exercises his authority to "purify all foods" (7:19).

Each half of these two parallel revelations ends with the story of a cure that is found only in the Gospel of Mark. First, in the case of the deaf-mute (7:31-37), Mark points to the mighty deeds of Jesus as revealing the arrival of messianic times by describing the man cured in terms used in Isaiah to portray their freedom: The "one incapable of speech" will speak (7:32, referring to Isa 35:5). Second, the cure of the blind man in stages by Jesus as he approaches Bethsaida is often seen as symbolic of the gradual enlightenment of the disciples of Jesus about the nature of his messiahship (8:22-26).

Rejection (8:28-30). The final scene in that third cycle describes the witness of Peter. Here is a case where knowledge of the structure of the writing as a whole is crucial for interpretation. When read in the context of these three cycles, which Mark has carefully constructed, the action of Peter is clearly a rejection of Jesus.

The incident describes a crisis in the ministry of Jesus. He recognizes that he has failed to make true disciples of the Galileans. So he retreats with his chosen companions into the Gentile region of Caesarea Philippi to the north. On the road he asks for their opinion about how the crowds look upon him. His disciples report the rumors going around. Readers recognize that all these opinions are wrong.

Jesus then wants to know whether his apostles have learned his true identity from their contacts with him. Peter confidently proclaims, "You are the Messiah" (8:30). Isn't that true? No, because it comes from using wrong criteria of evaluation. Jesus rejects the answer by telling them not to make any statements about him. His reaction is a demonstration of the messianic secret. Jesus knows that Peter is not yet able to recognize the true meaning of his role as Messiah.

Immediately the tone of the Gospel changes. Jesus knows that he must change his way of teaching and revealing. From that moment he turns his attention to this small group of willing but still unperceiving followers. They still judge him on the basis of their political expectations. They dream of the restoration of the kingdom of David.

Jesus has another vision of how he must carry out his mission. He starts to reveal his true destiny to the apostles. The remainder of the Gospel of Mark will concentrate on Jesus' efforts to purify and elevate the understanding of this core group. He reveals that he is the suffering Messiah and that they must share the mystery of the cross.

Stage Two:
Revelation of Jesus as Suffering Messiah (8:31–10:52)

Abruptly the Gospel of Mark takes a new direction. Jesus is aware that the Jewish people are not ready to accept him and his revelation. They desire the "old wine," that is, to remain within the Mosaic covenant (see 2:22). Nevertheless, Jesus determines to press forward to the completion of his mission and to leave the results in God's hands.

Since Mark entitles his work "the start of the good news," he sees the earthly ministry of Jesus as only the opening stage of God's revelation in him, who is now in glory as risen Son of God. Up to this point in Mark's story, Jesus has urged the crowds to repent and enter the kingdom of God. Now Jesus begins to identify himself regularly by a new title, "Son of Man." He invites the Twelve to follow as he begins the prophet's journey to Jerusalem and the cross.

This is not an easy journey to undertake. To stress that the difficulties are many, Mark pictures Jesus as presenting this invitation three times. In this part of the Gospel, Mark again makes use of the cycle technique in portraying the challenge of the cross (8:31–9:30; 9:31–10:32; 10:33-52). These cycles center around three predictions of the passion of Jesus and the impact they have on his disciples of all times.

The First Passion Prediction (8:31)

Immediately after Peter tries to put Jesus into the mold of a political king, Mark pictures Jesus formulating the first prediction of how his ministry is going to turn out. He is going to be rejected by the highest Jewish religious and political authorities and be executed. Yet God will not abandon him; Jesus will rise from the dead "after three days" (8:31). Such a fate lies beyond the power of Peter's imagination to grasp. He takes Jesus aside and chides him for thinking that such an event could happen. Jesus publicly rebuffs Peter's narrow point of view by calling him "Satan," that is, adversary of God's saving plan.

It is in carrying out this part of God's plan that Jesus will play the role of the "Son of Man," a phrase recalling the heavenly vision of the apocalyptic Book of Daniel in 7:9-14.

The term "Son of Man" begs for an explanation because it grew out of a Jewish movement not familiar to modern readers, the apocalyptic movement. After the Davidic kings had been overthrown by the Babylonians and the Jewish leaders had been driven into exile, the chosen people went through a long period of suffering and oppression. Even after they were allowed to go back to Jerusalem, the Jews were still under the domination of foreign states.

During the second century B.C.E., when they were an occupied nation, some Jews developed a new form of theology to encourage hope among themselves. They projected the final victory of the Lord over his enemies into the future as the dawn of a new age. This theology is called apocalyptic. It is found in the Book of Daniel, written about two hundred years before the preaching of Jesus, and in other Jewish writings popular at the time of Jesus.

The vision of the Son of Man in Daniel provided hope that God would send his people an agent of liberation. In adopting this mode of identification, Jesus focuses on qualities that set him apart from earthly political ambitions, and he identifies with those who have trusted in God's care for his people and saving activity in the world.

To drive home the serious implications of his courageous decision to trust in God's rule, Jesus gives a short summary of the conditions necessary for being his disciple (Mark 8:34–9:1). This instruction consists of only six items, arranged in two sets of three statements, balanced in reverse (chiasmic) order. In other words, statement 1 balances statement 6; statement 2 balances 5, and 3 balances 4, both in style and in content.

The message of statements 3 and 4 is that humans cannot buy their way into the kingdom of God by any personal skill or accomplishment. Jesus warns them not to jeopardize their eternal happiness by foolish trust in self (8:36-37). Statements 2 and 5 warn against trying to reach the kingdom by being self-serving (8:35, 38). Only trust in Jesus and fidelity to the gospel keep persons open to the gift of the kingdom.

The first statement extols the cross as the source of strength to sustain believers on the journey of life (8:34). As a balance to this affirmation, the final statement is surely ironic. Only the arrival of the Son of Man in glory will be dramatic enough to arouse the indifferent hearers to risk all for the kingdom (9:1). Jesus shows himself a realist!

In the following scene, as if to show that God's kingdom does have power, Mark records the transfiguration experience of Jesus, witnessed by Peter, James, and John (9:2-8). The miracle of the cure of the young man possessed by a devil, which Jesus performs after his disciples are unable to help, spells out his appeal for trust in God. "This kind cannot be driven out except by prayer" (9:29).

The Second Passion Prediction (9:31)

The second prediction of the fate of Jesus is stated in a more emphatic way by being put into the vivid historical present: "The Son of Man is being betrayed into human hands" (9:31). It is as if the event is already in progress. Even this dramatic prediction completely eludes the disciples, who start arguing about which one of them is going to be most important in the kingdom (9:34).

Once more Jesus takes the Twelve aside and instructs them about the nature of leadership in God's rule. It is achieved by becoming the least, by putting self at the disposal of others. Jesus uses the example of an infant. The disciples must be ready to serve the kingdom as totally as one engaged in caring for a baby.

The remainder of this cycle is filled with a variety of pieces of advice in order to spell out this attitude of humble service. Commentators see the topics as mirroring problems faced by the primitive Church. This variety of advice reflects the kinds of demands being made upon Christians in the community of Mark. For example, the effort to carry out responsibilities of the kingdom of God demands daily fidelity to the marriage partner (10:1-12) and detachment from earthly wealth (10:17-27).

Third Passion Prediction (10:33-34)

Jesus' third prediction of his rejection, death, and divine vindication comes at the dramatic moment when he is about to begin his journey to Jerusalem. As a prophet, Jesus knows that he is going to be betrayed and put to death. This prediction is stated in greater detail, as if incorporating the Church's memory of the passion Jesus endured. Again the disciples manifest callous disregard for the sufferings awaiting their leader. James and John ignore everything except the fact that he will "rise up" again. Perhaps they look upon the whole prediction only in figurative terms and latch on to its triumphal aspect to plead for special roles in what they interpret as a political victory over Rome.

Once more Jesus must redirect their perspective on the nature of his Father's rule in the world. The other apostles show that they share the same selfish attitude by becoming indignant that James and John might get better positions (10:40). For the third time Jesus gives a brief instruction on the nature of leadership in the kingdom as the antithesis of earthly power.

The one who wishes to be great in the kingdom must become servant (one who waits on tables), and whoever wants to be first will do so by becoming slave of all. Why is this necessary? "The Son of Man came not to be served but to serve and to give his life as a ransom for many" (10:45). This striking image is echoed in 1 Timothy 2:6 in describing the way Jesus acts as mediator before God on our behalf. The First Letter of John uses the image of Jesus as a sacrifice of propitiation for our sins in order to express the same activity of offering his life as ransom out of love for us (1 John 4:10).

At this point Jesus is in Jericho in the Jordan valley, ready to begin his ascent to Jerusalem and to death. He performs one final cure, the restoring of sight to the blind Bartimaeus, who immediately follows "along the way" (10:46-52). His example at this critical moment serves to illustrate for readers what true discipleship means—going wherever Jesus goes.

The Problem of Historical Reliability

When these narratives of the Gospel of Mark are examined as has been done here, their composition and organization as creative literary compositions emerges clearly. Naturally the question arises among modern readers, Did these events actually happen? This question arises out of our modern historical self-consciousness, a condition that was unknown to the evangelists.

Mark wrote as voice of the apostolic Church to bring future ages to a deep personal faith in Jesus. His Gospel makes use of rhetorical techniques for composing narratives that will guide readers in responding to the fidelity of Jesus to his mission.

Jesus' complete acceptance of God's will is what eventually draws him into confrontation with Jewish leaders and into rejection and death. The three passion predictions are Mark's way of proclaiming that Jesus is increasingly aware of human opposition. Yet he does not falter in obedience to the vision of his mission to proclaim the kingdom of God. Mark uses the resources of faith and rhetoric to construct a narrative with the kind of impact and appeal that will draw readers to a decision to bear witness to the kingdom of God.

Stage Three: The Final Week in Jerusalem (11:1-16:8)

The final third of Mark's Gospel describes the last week of the earthly Jesus. For Mark, in contrast with John, this is the only time that Jesus spends in Jerusalem during his public ministry. This historical discrepancy once again indicates that the Gospels do not provide a chronicle of all events in the life of Jesus on earth.

Even after Jesus enters the holy city of Jerusalem in triumph, he is forced to leave at night and seek safety in the neighboring village of Bethany (11:11). He returns the next day to purify the Temple and to restore it to its role as a "house of prayer" (11:17). In this sacred setting, Jesus gives his disciples instructions on faith and prayer. He promises that whatever they ask for with faith is already theirs. Although the Lord's Prayer is not recorded in Mark's Gospel, Jesus alludes to it when he warns his disciples against praying to their heavenly Father without forgiving their neighbors (11:25).

During this final week, Jesus displays divine wisdom by outsmarting his opponents in a series of ripostes (11:27–12:37). His final public statement is a word of praise for the poor widow, who has contributed her entire financial resources for that day (her daily "welfare check") to the upkeep of the Temple (12:41-44).

At this point we expect the Gospel of Mark to begin the narrative of the passion of Jesus, which occupies chapters 14 and 15 and which will be treated below in chapter 9. However, the Gospel takes an unexpected turn.

The Role of the Apocalyptic Discourse (13:1-37)

Here Mark inserts the second of the two lengthy discourses of his Gospel, an apocalyptic revelation that Jesus gives privately to four of his twelve apostles. To interpret this sermon, two preliminary steps are necessary: (1) to understand the nature of apocalyptic language, and (2) to determine why this discourse occurs at this point.

1. Apocalyptic as a literary genre for revealing future interventions of God flourished among the Jews from about 200 B.C.E. to 200 C.E. It is marked by characteristic features of form and content.

As to form, most apocalypses include a heavenly mediator acting as communicator of the revelation, usually through visions. As to content, they portray a final judgment of God upon history with rewards for the good and punishment for evil. The rewards are bestowed at the end of this age and usher the good into the new age, where God reigns without opposition.

2. What role does this apocalyptic passage play here? Mark inserts it as the first part of his portrayal of the divine vindication of Jesus. This prediction serves to balance his stark portrayal of the earthly sufferings of Jesus by widening the horizons of readers to the saving effects of his passion and death.

The vision of the ongoing turmoil that will surround the fall of Jerusalem instructs believers about the effects of rejecting the plan of God. The message remains valid for all readers until the present world passes away and the Son of Man appears in great power and glory as universal judge. It is, first of all, a reminder that all believers are involved in the passion of Jesus and must be on guard not to prove traitors. Those who wish to participate in the fruits of his death must heed his warning: "Watch" (13:37).

In addition, this sermon assures readers that the saving power of the unselfish offering of Jesus is operative now. Believers live in the apocalyptic era that began with the cosmic event of his death amid the darkness of Calvary (15:33). To benefit by that offering as a "ransom," disciples need to cultivate a spirit of faith and to watch and wait for the coming of the Lord in the face of opposition from this world (13:33-36).

The Dramatic Ending of Mark (16:8)

One surprise for many readers of a critical edition of the Gospel of Mark is its abrupt ending after the discovery of the empty tomb by the women (16:8). When they come to the tomb at daybreak on Easter morning, they find it empty. A young man in bright clothing calms their fears and reminds them of the promise of Jesus that he will go before his disciples into Galilee (16:7, referring to 14:28). But the women are seized with "trembling and confusion. And they said nothing to anyone, for they were afraid" (16:8).

This anticlimactic ending failed to satisfy the tastes of Christians after the Gospels of Matthew and Luke were written with their postresurrection appearances of Jesus. So early believers filled in the gap in the Gospel of Mark with a longer "canonical" ending. This simply gives a summary of the appearances of Jesus as found in the other three Gospels. This longer ending of Mark is part of the Church's official text of the New Testament and is accepted by believers as inspired. Yet it is not part of the original plan of Mark.

For Mark, the risen Lord in glory invites his disciples to journey to him. He gives them confidence and encourages them to faithful discipleship as they face all the obstacles he has warned them about in the apocalyptic discourse of chapter 13. Ultimately, response to the invitation to committed discipleship is the goal that Mark seeks to help his readers achieve. His writing, as he says in his title, is only the "start" of the good news. The gospel is the subsequent journey, first of Jesus and then of his disciples, toward the kingdom of God.

FOLLOW UP

As the most primitive Gospel, Mark is easier to study in terms of its story line. The shaping principle of gospel form lies near the surface and can easily be followed amid the progression of events. Many elements of primitive oral tradition survive in Mark. Attentive readers can follow his skillful integration of various traditions by his summaries and dramatic style in this vibrant picture of Jesus as proclaiming the arrival of the kingdom of God.

Modern readers of Mark are also challenged to follow key themes, like his Christology, his emphasis on the silence of Jesus (the messianic secret), his unfolding of the cost of discipleship. The ultimate way to celebrate "the good news of Jesus Christ, Son of God," is to take up the cross and undertake the journey of discipleship.

Helpful material for entering into this journey can be found in the variety of commentaries on Mark now available. Readers will decide the depth of detail they wish to pursue. A recent commentary addressed to educated lay believers is Wilfrid Harrington, *Mark* (Wilmington, Del.: Michael Glazier, 1979).

For focus on the rhetoric of Mark from a variety of points of view, readers can consult David Rhoads and Donald Michie, *Mark as Story: An Introduction to the Narrative of a Gospel* (Philadelphia: Fortress, 1982). More stress on various methods and theological themes is given in Carol Walters, Jr., *I, Mark: A Personal Encounter* (Atlanta: John Knox, 1980).

5

Matthew: The Preacher's Guide

As with the Gospel of Mark, the first step in studying Matthew is to read his Gospel rapidly several times. Even this naive approach should be enough to convince a reader that Matthew represents a development in the evolution of the literary genre called "gospel." In addition to the story line created by Mark, Matthew incorporates a large amount of discourse material in the form of long sermons attributed to Jesus as well as extensive polemic between Jesus and Jewish leaders.

Because the Gospel of Matthew contains an abundance of discourse as well as narration, it is more difficult than Mark to grasp and analyze. By setting this extended discourse material in tension with the story line, Matthew challenges readers to a greater use of literary and theological imagination in entering into dialogue with Jesus. In fact, some commentators go so far as to say that Matthew has adopted a new shaping principle for his work and has thus transformed gospel genre into a different literary form. I disagree and accept Matthew as a true gospel.

The overarching approach of this chapter will help readers follow Matthew's carefully organized presentation. It is simply a more elaborate development of the shaping principle of gospel described in chapter 3. In this expansion Matthew introduces features that make his writing a more effective teaching tool and a popular text for public reading in Church liturgy.

Why did the unknown author of the Gospel of Matthew feel the need of expanding the form created by Mark and the early

Christian community? Without presuming to formulate the author's intention, modern readers find sufficient indications in the text to affirm that it was shaped to respond to changing needs and situations within the growing Jewish Christian communities.

After the colorful Markan narrative had been read for several years in public worship, younger members of the communities, who had no personal experience of the earthly Jesus, wanted to hear more about the biographical details of their risen Lord. Christians were being excluded from rabbinical synagogues and needed to deepen their rootedness in the Jewishness of Jesus. They wanted to hear about places connected with his origin and to find out more about his teaching. The response to these needs was the addition of an infancy gospel and of more sermon material in the Gospel of Matthew.

The Infancy Gospel of Jesus Immanuel (1:1–2:23)

The Gospel of Matthew devotes only forty-eight verses to the childhood of Jesus. These include a stylized genealogy that links Jesus to the two most important figures in Israel's history, namely, Abraham and David. The first part of this genealogy simplifies lists of Israelite ancestors of David found in Jewish Scriptures. As the genealogy approaches Jesus, it passes beyond the Old Testament period and incorporates names not found in the Hebrew Bible.

Matthew also introduces a striking feature into this genealogy by calling attention to the names of foreign women among the ancestors of Jesus, namely, Tamar and Ruth (1:3, 5). These names anticipate Jesus' concern for sinners and outcasts and prepare readers for the Christian Church's outreach to all peoples of the earth, ordered in the final scene (28:16-20).

A more significant feature of this genealogy is the comment Matthew adds to it (1:17). He invites readers to reflect on the division of the genealogy into three sets of fourteen generations, something highly dubious from a historical point of view. The division focuses attention on the role of David as fulfillment of the promises given to Abraham and then on the fall of his dynasty during the Babylonian captivity. But unexpectedly, in another fourteen generations (actually thirteen, to call attention to the mysterious birth of Jesus to the Virgin Mary) the Messiah is born. This pattern alerts readers that Jesus is the true David, a name that has the numerical value of fourteen in Hebrew letters. This genealogy thus introduces Jesus as transcendent king and ongoing fulfillment of God's promises to Abraham.

The remainder of the infancy gospel of Matthew contains only three short accounts (1:18-25; 2:1-18; 2:19-23). These identify Jesus as (1) born of the Virgin Mary, (2) incorporated into the kingly line of David by Joseph's willingness to acknowledge him as his son, and (3) born in the Davidic city of Bethlehem during the reign of Herod the Great.

Matthew illustrates the universal kingship of Jesus by means of the scene of the wise magicians from the East directed to the new king by his star (2:2). Their coming creates terror for Herod, who tries to kill this apparent rival. When an angel warns Joseph, Jesus is taken to safety in Egypt. Readers will not miss the irony of Jesus' finding safety in the land of Israel's traditional enemy. After the death of Herod, Joseph settles in Nazareth to fulfill the cryptic reference to "the prophets" (2:23), which will be explained in terms of a feature of Matthew's Gospel, the formula quotations.

The Ten Formula Quotations

Within the infancy gospel of Matthew appear four quotations from the Hebrew Scriptures in the form of comments by Matthew on specific events in the life of Jesus as fulfilling Scripture. These four are part of a set of ten quotations that are characteristic of Matthew. They are all introduced by a special formula. Matthew inserts them as kind of footnotes to explain that specific events in the life of Jesus fulfill the passage that he then quotes from Scripture. These ten passages are:

1:22-23. The birth of Immanuel fulfills the Greek text of Isaiah 7:14 to explain the virgin birth of Jesus.

2:15. The return of Jesus from Egypt fulfills Hosea 11:1, the text announcing the Exodus as God's calling his Son from Egypt.

2:17-18. The slaughter of the children in Bethlehem fulfills the wailing of Rachel when the inhabitants of Ramah were murdered, as told in Jeremiah 31:15.

2:23. When Joseph decides to settle in Nazareth, Matthew pictures the move as fulfilling "what was spoken through the prophets," namely, that Jesus should be called a "Nazorean." This quotation baffles modern readers when they look for the reference and discover that the city of Nazareth is never mentioned in Hebrew Scriptures. Certainly Matthew knew that also. So what does this footnote mean? It is an example of a rabbinic technique that clarifies a situation through a cryptic allusion to Scripture.

The technique here is a play on words. Hebrew has two words that sound like Nazareth. One means a "Nazorite," a person consecrated to God, like the liberator Samson. The other means "shoot" of a plant, a term describing David in Isaiah 11:1. Readers familiar with this technique would make the connection with one or both texts. This esoteric use of rabbinic scholarship illustrates that all these quotations are the fruit of a prayerful searching of the Jewish Bible by the school of Matthew.

4:14-16. When Jesus sets up preaching headquarters in Capernaum, he fulfills Isaiah 8:23–9:1, because the light of his preaching reverses the effect of the Assyrian invasion in the territories of Naphtali and Zebulun hundreds of years before.

8:17. Jesus' miraculous cures accomplish the redemptive role of the Suffering Servant of Isaiah 53:4.

12:17-21. The healings of Jesus identify him as fulfilling the role of the loyal servant chosen by God to give hope to the nations in Isaiah 42:1-4.

13:35. Jesus' method of revealing the kingdom through parables fulfills the proverb of the prophet who wrote Psalm 78:2, that the mysteries hidden from the beginning of the world are now proclaimed.

21:4-7. When Jesus rides into Jerusalem on an ass and her colt, he fulfills the ideal of the meek messianic ruler who is pictured here by Matthew's combining Isaiah 62:10 and Zechariah 9:9.

27:9-10. This composite quotation is formed by weaving passages from Jeremiah, especially 32:6-10, and Zechariah 11:12-13. Again Matthew uses rabbinic technique to explain events surrounding the death of Judas as pointing to the hope of redemption through the saving blood of Jesus.

By collecting and integrating these ten learned rabbinic-style reflections into his Gospel, Matthew has employed an apologetic technique appealing to his primary audience, Jewish Christians and the "godfearers," that is, Gentiles attracted to the Jewish Scriptures and morals. These quotations provide a comprehensive justification for their faith in Jesus. Ten is a symbolic number for completeness. These are not meant to provide a rational motive for credibility but an expression of the deep faith of early Jewish Christians.

These quotations illustrate what Jesus says in the first part of the Sermon on the Mount: he came not to destroy "the law and the prophets" but to "fulfill" them (5:17). They show how Matthew conceives salvation history. Through the life and mission of Jesus, the plan of God achieves a new level of saving "justice," a term found in the Gospel seven times (the number that symbolizes perfection).

The Great Sermons of Matthew's Gospel

The most striking modification of the shaping principle of the gospel genre in this Gospel is the introduction of six long discourse sections into the story of the ministry of Jesus as found in the Gospel of Mark. Matthew portrays Jesus as opening up his public ministry with a comprehensive sermon to outline the morality of the kingdom of God. Before analyzing that magnificent discourse, I will list the six long sermons in which Matthew systematizes the instructions Jesus gives to his followers as a whole or to their leaders:

The Sermon on the Mount (5:1–7:29). A comprehensive overview of the greater justice revealed by the kingdom of God.

The Mission Sermon (10:5–11:1). Addressed to the Twelve, who are called apostles only in the insert introducing this instruction. It synthesizes a variety of advice on how the kingdom is to be proclaimed and how its preachers are to conduct themselves.

The Parable Sermon (13:1-53). A structured collection of six parables about the nature of the "kingdom of heaven," as Matthew prefers to call it. These are introduced by the parable of the sower, a parable that shows how to hear the word of God.

Sermon for Leaders of a Divided Community (18:2–19:2). A set of admonitions to the Twelve on how to deal with different types of situations that threaten to split the believing community.

Prophetic Controversies in Jerusalem (21:23–23:39). A collection of disputes, prophetic laments (woes), and parables that display Jesus' final confrontation with hostile Jewish leaders. Most commentators do not list the composite collection as a major sermon of Matthew because it does not end with the standard formula that closes the other five.

The Apocalyptic Sermon (24:3–25:46). A portrayal of the fall of Jerusalem, which points to the end of this age. In response to questions from his disciples, Jesus predicts the destruction of Jerusalem and the coming of the Son of Man in glory as judge of this sinful age. Matthew balances the predictions, which are similar to those in Mark, by adding a series of six parables, three long and three short. These exhort readers to prepare for these events and for the final judgment, which will be conducted by the glorious Son of Man.

The Sermon on the Mount and the Miracle Section (5:1–9:38)

Only Matthew pictures Jesus as summarizing his ethical vision in one comprehensive sermon. As a teacher, he places this summary at the beginning of the public ministry of Jesus. This location is pedagogical rather than historical in that it addresses the needs of readers rather than reflect the career of Jesus. The text of this magnificent sermon, including its brief introduction and conclusion, extends over three chapters, for a total of ninety-seven verses.

It begins with a series of blessings (the "Beatitudes"), a literary form common in Jewish Scripture although never in the litany form found here. The arrangement suggests that Matthew sees these nine blessings as replacing the Ten Commandments of the Sinai covenant inaugurated by Moses. The Beatitudes point to the new covenant rooted in the death of Jesus.

Moses gave a series of limit commandments, fixing boundaries beyond which faithful Israelites "shall not" go. In a striking contrast, Jesus offers members of the new covenant a series of goal commands to guide their conduct toward the fullness of the saving justice of the kingdom of God. Jesus says he has come not to destroy "the law or the prophets," but rather to fulfill them (5:17). The Sermon on the Mount outlines for believers the justice of that kingdom as (1) fuller, (2) purer, (3) more effective, than the justice of the Law of Moses.

Fuller Justice. The ideal of fuller justice is spelled out in the form of six contrasts between what Jesus wants of his followers and the prescriptions of the Mosaic Law (5:21-48). Instead of simply limiting evil, like murder, adultery, perjury, and revenge, Jesus directs his followers to cultivate a dynamic life-style of forgiveness, reconciliation, self-control, unwavering fidelity to the original marriage partner, absolute truthfulness in all communication, refusal to join in any kind of evil conduct, and a determination to support every other human being, even as God does in his mercy.

Purer Justice. The purer justice of the kingdom of God manifests itself in the three principal ascetical practices of the Law of Moses: almsgiving, prayer, and fasting (6:1-18). In the Sermon on the Mount, these practices are understood in their general sense of responsible conduct toward fellow human beings, toward God, and in personal growth. Setting them forth in parallel passages says that one's neighbor's needs are as real as one's own and call for equal concern.

In the directions on prayer, Matthew inserts the Lord's Prayer as exemplary of the purer justice believers exercise in praising God by practicing reconciliation. The new, holistic vision of the kingdom as revealing God's glory and universal saving will is the heart of true worship. From that form of prayer flows true fasting as integrated self-control, devoting believers totally to "the will of my Father in heaven" (7:21). The transcendent orientation of the kingdom in no way distracts the followers of Jesus from being fully involved in the daily life of the community and of the world.

More Effective Justice. The Sermon on the Mount uses a variety of activities and images to portray the effective justice of the kingdom of God. These are elaborated in the remainder of the Sermon (6:19–7:27).

Believers reject the worship of "Mammon," which is the personification of wealth, because to serve wealth is a form of idolatry. Effective justice means absolute trust in God, single-minded devotion, sympathetic understanding, prudence—in a word, the grounding of one's entire life in the appeal of God to renounce all for the kingdom.

Intimately connected to the Sermon on the Mount is the following carefully constructed narrative. It celebrates the authority of Jesus as Messiah by describing ten of his mighty deeds, half of the miraculous cures recorded in the Gospel of Matthew (8:1–9:34). This wide-ranging display of power over all forms of sickness and demonic domination prove that Jesus is the chosen one of God who proclaims the arrival of the kingdom.

The crowds admire Jesus because he is "teaching them as one endowed with power" (7:29). Now this healing ministry proves that his power is a gift of God. The mighty deeds of Jesus will be treated all together later, in chapter 8. Within this miracle section Matthew includes two scenes on the responsibility of disciples to direct their whole life to the kingdom. The call of Matthew is one of those scenes (9:9-13). It is an occasion for celebration but also a warning that the cost of discipleship is continuous and demanding (9:14-17).

The Mission Discourse and Challenges of Jesus (10:1–12:50)

The Gospel of Matthew continues to unfold in a carefully orchestrated way. The teaching and healing power of Jesus, which announces the kingdom, also reveals profound needs on the part of the hearers (9:36). So Jesus assembles the Twelve, imparts to them his power over evil spirits, and lays out a missionary agenda (10:5-42). This instruction is obviously suited for the leaders of Matthew's own community.

Why then does Jesus tell the disciples to restrict their mission work to "the lost sheep of the house of Israel" (10:6)? This paradox is reflected in the activities following these instructions. The disciples do not go forth to heal and preach but remain with Jesus, who continues "to teach and proclaim in their towns" (11:1). Although the earthly Jesus confines his ministry to Israel, after his postresurrection commission his followers will reach out to all nations (28:19).

The way Jesus conducts himself provokes the imprisoned John the Baptizer to send a delegation to ask the meaning of his gentle treatment of sinners. Jesus justifies his approach by appealing to the prophecy of Isaiah (35:5-6). In the messianic times the poor would be healed and set free (11:5-6).

At this point Jesus begins to adopt a more hostile tone toward various groups. This hostility appears in the "woes," or prophetic laments (a kind of anti-Beatitudes), against the three cities of Galilee that have closed themselves to his teaching (11:21). This hostility will intensify until Jesus delivers a series of seven "woes" against the scribes and Pharisees in Jerusalem (23:13-36).

Yet Jesus also urges his followers to trust in his Father, "Lord of the whole universe," who has given him the mission of going out to "those who toil and are oppressed" (11:25-30). This prayer shows that Jesus is conscious of fulfilling the Father's saving justice by proclaiming himself "greater than the Temple" (12:42). Jesus proclaims that the prophet expressed God's will: "I prefer mercy to ritual offering" (Hos 6:6). That is, God has sent Jesus to bring to fulfillment the ideals planted in the heart of Israel by Moses and the prophets.

This fidelity of Jesus to his mission provides the basis for the seventh fulfillment quotation. Matthew celebrates Jesus as the Suffering Servant described by Isaiah. God's Spirit rests on Jesus. He offers hope to all peoples, because his loving obedience is a source of hope to the oppressed (12:17-21).

That reflection alerts readers that they are called to choose to serve the kingdom of God. As Jesus puts it, "The one who is not with me is against me" (12:30). The growing resistance to Jesus is expressed in Matthew's repetition of key words and phrases like "that brand" of persons (12:41 and 23:36); "brood of vipers" (12:34 and 23:33); "this wicked and adulterous generation seeks a sign" (12:39 and 16:4). Jesus challenges his own relatives when he says that they can be joined to him only by doing "the will of my Father in heaven" (12:50).

Parable Sermon and
Foreshadowing of the Church (13:1–17:27)

Only at this point, almost the center of his Gospel, does Matthew insert for the first time explicit narrative parables of Jesus. As usual, he collects a symbolic number (seven), beginning with the parable of the seed. With it, he records the traditional explanation from oral tradition. The parable is about hearing the word of God. He follows up with six parables that reveal aspects of the kingdom of God. These parables will be treated together with other parables of Jesus in the next chapter.

Once again, the narratives that follow this major sermon illustrate its key themes. Matthew here focuses on how Jesus forms his chosen Twelve into the guiding force destined to lead the Church after the resurrection. As the crowds become more anxious to profit by the gifts that Jesus possesses, he becomes more disillusioned with their motives. He devotes his energies almost exclusively to preparing his chosen disciples, especially Peter, for their mission.

Jesus demonstrates his power to supply the needs of those who come to him (11:28). Twice he feeds those who come to hear him in deserted places (14:13-21; 15:32-39). Both of these feedings are told in the form of a liturgy of thanksgiving. They include a blessing of God, a distribution of the loaves, and a careful gathering of the fragments. The Twelve participate in a special way in these marvelous feedings, which prepare them for the institution of the Eucharist at the Last Supper.

Several narratives of Matthew 14–17 focus on Peter. After the first multiplication of the loaves, Jesus sends the Twelve across the lake and then comes to them at night walking across the water. Peter recognizes Jesus and asks to join him walking on the waves. Jesus invites him to come, but Peter soon loses confidence in the face of strong winds. Jesus has to reach out to this person "of little faith" (14:28-31). The small community in prayer in the rocking boat symbolizes the Church, which worships its Lord amid human adversity.

In the scene at Caesarea Philippi where Peter replies to the question of Jesus about his identity, he displays his postresurrection faith, in contrast to his response in the Gospel of Mark (16:13-18;

see Mark 8:29). Peter professes that Jesus is "the Christ, the Son of the living God." This profession of faith earns the change of his name from Simon into Peter, the rock upon whom Jesus will build the Church, impregnable against the domination of the nether world, Hades. Scenes like this win for Matthew's Gospel the title of "Church Gospel" and make it popular for reading in the liturgy.

This new role does not immediately eliminate Peter's earthly ambition. When Jesus goes on to predict that he must suffer and be put to death, Peter objects. Jesus should get rid of such foolish ideas. Jesus angrily turns on Peter and addresses him as "Satan," adversary. Peter puts himself in the same category as the devil, who had tried earlier to divert Jesus from his God-given mission (16:21-23).

Peter also plays an important part in the scene of the transfiguration of Jesus. Overwhelmed by the appearance of Moses and Elijah and by the shining face of Jesus, Peter wants to commemorate this divine appearance by erecting a shrine, as the patriarchs of Israel had done. Jesus rejects this suggestion and orders the three participants not to speak of this event until he is risen from the dead (17:4-9). Peter is privileged to act as agent for Jesus in paying the Temple tax for both of them, an obligation Jesus fulfills as a loyal Jew who respects God's holy dwelling (17:24-27).

Instructions for Church Leaders (18:1–23:39)

Readers of the Gospel of Matthew can feel the tensions between Jesus and the Jewish leadership increase as Jesus prepares his disciples for his betrayal and death. The more his mission isolates Jesus from the religious leadership, the more he concentrates on preparing leaders for the Church for which Matthew is writing. The evangelist employs three literary techniques to communicate his gospel portrait of Jesus:

Schematizing. Compared to the Gospel of Mark, the narrative portions of Matthew are usually schematic. Matthew eliminates as many descriptive details as possible and almost turns his characters into types. His story line reads like a summary that serves as model for the conduct of readers.

Synthesizing. Matthew is at pains to give a clear account of the message of Jesus. His long sermons provide an orderly presentation of the teaching of Jesus, and his editorial inserts help readers to avoid any misunderstanding. He groups the ideals that Jesus preached into a litany of striking blessings, the Beatitudes that synthesize the moral norms that believers strive for. His parable chapter offers a synthesis of the qualities of the kingdom of God.

Systematizing. Matthew has carefully collected the key elements of the teaching of Jesus into a set of systematic sermons, beginning with the general outline of new covenant moral conduct in the Sermon on the Mount. Once Jesus has picked the first leaders of the new community, Matthew presents him as giving them and their successors a practical missionary agenda. In these and other ways, his Gospel displays a variety of rhetorical techniques to increase the impact and appeal of his presentation. He drives home the truth that the Church continues the work of Jesus, to fulfill the Law and the Prophets.

These skillful literary devices provide links between the Church community for which Matthew writes and the earthly Jesus, who lived more than a generation before. He devotes his fourth great sermon to offer special advice to the leaders of his own community in the spirit of Jesus.

How can Church leaders now best exercise their authority on behalf of the kingdom of God? Rather than striving for honors as if they were rivals or political rulers, Jesus invites leaders of his Church to become "like children" (18:3). They are to put aside all personal ambition and rely totally upon the power of God at work in them. Only when they recognize that they cannot establish the kingdom of God by human wisdom and skill are they able to celebrate it as gift and grace.

In particular, Christian leaders are to place themselves at the service of all, just as Jesus did. He so identified with the weak that leaders of his Church cannot continue his mission without being totally available. By graphic images and examples, Jesus spells out the responsibility of these leaders to protect the weak and vulnerable from sin and exploitation. The heavenly Father is the true shepherd, who does not want to lose any of his flock. Just as Jesus was willing to go to any length to guide his Father's little ones to salvation, so must his followers use their imagination to reach out to all in need.

Careful reading of this sermon (18:1-35) makes clear why it has been aptly designated as a sermon for leaders of a divided community. In writing, Matthew obviously mirrors the needs of his own community as it faces problems of adaptation. Its leaders must be ministers of reconciliation in face of divisive tensions. Peter's question about how often fellow members are to be forgiven brings a stirring call to generosity on the part of all involved by Jesus, "not seven but seventy-seven [or seven times seventy] times" (18:22). This openness to forgive is an earthly reflection of the Father's infinite compassion for all.

Jesus illustrates the power of forgiveness in the closing parable. The rich property-owner forgives totally at the plea of his helpless servant. Yet this pardon comes unraveled when the servant shows himself unbending to the needs of a fellow servant. Readers hear an echo of the prayer that Jesus taught them to pray, "forgive us as we forgive" (see 6:12).

The remainder of the ministry of Jesus as narrated by the Gospel of Matthew highlights increasingly bitter controversies with Jewish leaders. These exchanges will lead to the death of Jesus as a "ransom for many" (20:28). In face of stiffening resistance, Jesus creates further parables about the kingdom of God and vindicates his mode of acting by wise rejoinders.

When his words fall on deaf ears, Jesus takes the initiative and invokes the anger of the scribes and Pharisees by a series of prophetic oracles against them. He exposes them as hypocrites for oppressing God's people and perverting his will (23:13-33).

These words lead into Matthew's version of the apocalyptic discourse about punishments to come on Jerusalem and the whole world at the end of this age. To this sermon Jesus adds a set of three parables of watchfulness as well as warnings to his followers not to let down their guard against temptation. Thus, Matthew turns Mark's terrifying revelation into a message of hope with a brilliant finale. He paints a graphic vision of the Last Judgment by the Son of Man (25:31-46). It is a call to readers to live out of a strong faith in the power of the good news to overcome all evil. The response of faith does not remain idle but expresses itself in praise of God and service of his little ones.

FOLLOW UP

The systematic arrangement for the material in the Gospel of Matthew gives it a strong appeal. His careful linking of the pronouncements of Jesus with schematic narratives about his earthly mission invites readers to unite with the words and deeds of Jesus to seek the holiness and justice of the kingdom of God. A faithful reading evokes the power of its form and content upon members of the Church, through whom Jesus wants to make the power of the kingdom available to all nations.

The Church is called to be a community of the truly wise. Its leaders are scribes trained in the kingdom "to draw from its treasure the old and the new" (13:52). Once believers feel at home with the shaping principle of gospels, it is time for them to go deeper into the entire text.

A detailed commentary meant for interested and serious students of Matthew is John Meier, *Matthew* (Wilmington: Del.: Michael Glazier, 1980).

6

Parables Reveal the Kingdom

As I said in the first chapter, the Gospels are both faith documents and literary creations. They were composed in that style
of language that is called religious. Its purpose is not to inform
readers of facts about a God "out there." Rather, religious language invites humans to orient their lives and values to the God
who makes himself available as giver of freedom and salvation.

The Gospels reveal that God is making himself available to
humans in the risen Jesus as their final destiny. They originated
in a community that believed Jesus was still present in the world
as Lord of the new age. The Gospels do not speculate on how
deeply Jesus was aware of that mystery in his human consciousness during his life on earth.

Certainly the earthly Jesus was vividly aware that God was his
Father. He knew God was acting within him and through him
to exercise new saving power and presence in the world. In the
Synoptic Gospels Jesus often calls that divine presence "the kingdom of God." Matthew prefers the designation "kingdom of
heaven," because he adopts the Jewish custom of not mention-
ing the divine name. Heaven is a substitute for God.

The Synoptic Gospels picture Jesus as revealing the kingdom
and making it available chiefly by means of parables. They use
the term parable forty-eight times—Matthew, seventeen; Mark,
thirteen; and Luke, eighteen times.

In the Gospels the term "parable" describes a variety of language uses we do not ordinarily call "parable" in English. It

covers the spectrum from short proverbs to metaphors to full-length illustrations. For example, Luke calls parables sentences like "Physician, heal yourself" (4:23) and "The blind can't lead the blind, can they?" (6:39). Many New Testament commentators adopt this wide Jewish usage and call many gospel comparisons by the name parable.

Basically a parable is a metaphor, or comparison. It comes from a Greek word that means "thrown alongside." It always denotes a figurative use of language. Hence it implies a meaning deeper than that of the literal use of the words contained in it. A parable preserves the tension of meaning on two levels at the same time.

Because parables incorporate a double level of meaning, they always create challenges for readers. They remain open to different interpretations. Religious parables like those in the Synoptic Gospels stir up a response in readers, just as the preaching of Jesus evokes response from his hearers.

Why Jesus Spoke in Parables (Matthew 13:10-17)

If parables operate on more than one level at the same time, why did Jesus choose such a difficult literary form for revealing the kingdom of God? Why did he make them the ordinary vehicle of his preaching?

This question is not new; it arose in the early Church. In fact, it arose even before the Gospels. And they answered the question in a surprising way, namely, by preserving the variety of opinions about parables circulating in the early communities. Instead of choosing one answer, the evangelists incorporated current opinions about why Jesus used parables side by side with the parables themselves (see Mark 4:10-12; Matt 13:10-17; Luke 8:9-10).

Their solution tells us that the question has many answers. We can go further. It tells us that none of these answers gives the complete reason why Jesus spoke in parables. The reasons preserved by the Synoptics grew out of reflection by early believers on the impact and appeal of the revelation communicated by Jesus and the challenges it holds for believers.

The Synoptics gather these reflections about the purpose of parables in the form of paradoxical answers that Jesus gives for adopting this form of revelation. The answers occur between the parable of the sower as given by Jesus and its traditional explanation preserved by the oral preachers. The occasion for the explanation is the question of the disciples themselves. They want to know why Jesus adopts this unusual approach.

His answers links parables to outsiders. Jesus says, strangely, that he addresses parables only to outsiders, not to the disciples. That is, he speaks in parables to those who do not accept the mystery of the kingdom. The answer is a paradox, because Jesus also said he came to announce the kingdom and he spent his time going around preaching. Mark opens his version of the parable discourse with the note that Jesus "started to teach them many things in parables" (Mark 4:2).

Matthew enlarges Jesus' answer to the disciples about his use of parables. They are a form of fulfillment that enable the disciples to see and hear what the prophets were denied (13:16-17). He also inserts one of the ten fulfillment-formula quotations later into the sermon. He reminds his readers that Jesus taught in parables to fulfill the prophetic passage that he was destined to proclaim things hidden from the foundation of the world (13:35, citing Ps 78:2).

Why the variety of answers? Because the evangelists insert into the discourse the change of emphasis in the Church's use of parables in contrast with that of Jesus. The comment that the crowds did not understand the mystery of the kingdom looks to the actual result of the whole mission of Jesus at the time the Gospels were written. The Jewish people who refused to hear the teaching of Jesus and who expelled the first Christians from their synagogues are identified with the original crowds who rejected Jesus.

By the time the Gospels were written, the majority of the Jewish people had rejected the preaching of the apostles. In doing that, they identified themselves with the negative response their ancestors gave to the prophets. Matthew finds the word of the prophet being fulfilled in the rejection of Jesus and his Church by his own people.

At the same time, the Gospels show that this rejection pained Jesus. He faithfully carried out his mission as Messiah to reveal God's saving love and hoped to be heard. Parables played an important part in that revelation by forcing the crowds to decide for or against Jesus and the kingdom (see 13:52-53).

Parables as Revelation

Early Christians found it hard to understand the rejection of Jesus by his own people. It almost seemed as if the plan of God had failed! But their faith could not accept such a solution. Their desire to understand the rejection of Jesus impelled them to keep reflecting on the role that parables had in provoking the rejection of Jesus.

Parables were not a substitute for another method of revelation that was better. Jesus did not have recourse to them as a way to patronize ignorant peasants who did not understand spiritual realities. Those who walked miles to hear Jesus were religious people well acquainted with the Law of Moses and the Jewish Scriptures.

Jesus sympathized with the good will of his audiences and invited them to move closer to God's will than the Law of Moses could take them. He was anxious to share his own experience of the Father's power and love working within him. His role was not that of a human teacher stimulating native intelligence to master new material.

The revelation of Jesus was of a different nature. He came making available a living truth that shaped the lives of those who embraced his empowered vision. Would they drink the new wine or stay with the old as a better way of life? (Luke 7:33). Tragically, they chose the old. Mark notes that after the last parable that Jesus spoke in Jerusalem (the story of the wicked vineyardists), his opponents "knew that he spoke this parable against them" (Mark 12:12).

To bring about this soul-searching decision, a striking mode of speech was needed. The parables were the perfect literary vehicle for forcing hearers to accept or reject new life. It was a unique experience that generated these profound parables. They carried hearers beyond what they saw and heard each day into the world of Jesus.

No doubt Jesus, as he developed a parable, elaborated on individual elements and refined details to make the choice clear.

The Synoptic Gospels transmit them in an extremely condensed or dehydrated form. They survive only in the barest outline, which usually consists of three steps:

Revelation. Some aspect of the saving power of the kingdom of God. No one parable says everything, but each offers some facet that makes the kingdom available.

Revolution. The overthrowing of the old world of limited visions about God and his will. The parables of Jesus offer new possibilities and challenges.

Resolution. The call to radical newness. To enter this new world of the kingdom, one must leave behind the old world with its selfish or limited values.

The vivid images found in the parables of Jesus sprang from his superior powers of observation, which were totally at the disposal of his unique religious experience and commitment. He filled images familiar to his audiences with divine insight. All creation spoke to him of the kingdom: the nets used by Galilean fishermen, the kneading of bread, the hard lot of day laborers, the ambition of the rich, the growth of a fig tree.

Jesus was so in tune with the Spirit of God that he found in events of his social, economic, political, and religious experience images to portray elements of the kingdom of God. His parables are figurative expressions showing how these earthly events point beyond this world.

Reading his parables shows how Jesus compared the kingdom not to static elements but to activities. Gospel parables are dramatic narratives, stories that open onto the activity of the kingdom of God now at work. They reveal spiritual truth as dynamic power that invites to faith and conversion. Every parable, as a call to discipleship in the kingdom, becomes meaningful in producing a change of heart and life.

The ability of these minidramas to express his religious experience made them appropriate for Jesus. They show how he involved himself in the human condition to offer believers a share in God's gifts as their ultimate destiny. Their challenge is essential to their place in his revelation.

To enter this new world, which the parables of Jesus created, his hearers had to leave their present one behind. Most in his audience refused to do so. For them, the parables became condemnation rather than life. In the end, even the little they had would be taken away (Matt 25:29).

Parables as Miracles in Words

How did this dramatization of revelation's call to conversion and new life operate? Parables function as exercises of religious language. In them Jesus was not relating facts about the kingdom but evoking decisions for it. Parables enlighten and empower hearers to embrace the values and accept the demands of the kingdom.

In a real sense, parables operate as miracles in words because they enable hearers to entrust their destiny to God. This is the miracle of conversion. By his parables Jesus inspired in others the trust and vision that animated his own life. He deepened the faith and wisdom of receptive hearts to acknowledge saving truth and to choose it by their actions.

For those willing to admit their need for the kingdom and its power, the parables brought healing from alienation. They gave a sense of wholeness to life. The hope they communicated brought hearers a sense of being in touch with satisfying reality and truth. They opened up new possibilities for those who followed Jesus. He uprooted listeners from the self-centered love that destroys life. To choose to lose one's life for the kingdom is a miracle of healing and of hope (Matt 16:25).

This religious conversion embraces the plan of God as making sense out of the ambiguities of earthly existence. So parables make believers able and willing to enlist in the drama of salvation lovingly and joyfully. In this faith decision, those who follow Jesus become fully human, for they allow God to be their Savior and ruler of their destiny.

The Parable of the Sower
(Matt 13:3-9; Mark 4:3-9; Luke 8:4-8)

Each of the three Synoptics has a special parable discourse. Matthew greatly extends his version in keeping with his method of expanding the teaching of Jesus and grouping his material in a systematic way (Matt 13:1-52). Luke, on the contrary, greatly curtails this discourse in keeping with his practice of making sermons short (Luke 8:4-18). In Mark the parable sermon is the first extended discourse of Jesus (Mark 4:3-22).

Significantly, all three evangelists begin their sermon with the parable of the sower, and all include an explanation of it. To have an explanation of a parable is rare in the Synoptics. The unusual feature of this explanation is that it does not correspond exactly to the parable. The explanation deals with the fate of the seeds rather than with the sower.

The similarity of all three accounts indicates that this parable played a prominent role in early Christian preaching. Evidently, this common explanation grew up during the period of oral tradition, as preachers applied the actions of the parable to actual fruits of evangelization by the apostles and Christian prophets. Here again the Synoptics incorporate reaction to the ministry of early Christian preachers.

Is it possible to go back beyond the resurrection and grasp the parable of the sower in the context of the earthly life of Jesus? Yes. Commentators have done this by paying close attention to the words of the parable itself. I pointed out above that the question about teaching in parables (which follows the parable of the sower in all three Synoptics) refers to divisions between Jews and Christians. Christians were asking why so many Jews refused to accept the mystery of the resurrection.

An analysis of the parable of the sower shows that it is a parable about understanding parables. Jesus dramatizes the mystery of God's word calling to salvation. The story level is easy to grasp. Jesus describes details of a scene of planting by scattering the seed, as was customary in the Palestine of his day. It is a scene familiar to his hearers. On the second level, Jesus is speaking about his own ministry.

The real message of the parable lies on this second or metaphorical level. Jesus was not delivering a lecture on farming. He was revealing the fate of the ministry of his preaching. The original audience of Jesus could have drawn many religious messages from this parable.

Jesus saw himself as sowing the word of God, making it available to many hearts. The parable tells about the many tensions that his revelation created as it called the great range of hearers to conversion. There are many ways of not hearing and not responding to the kingdom at work in the ministry of Jesus.

Some hearers never even understand the demands of conversion. They do not allow the kingdom to receive a hearing in their heart. For them, conversion is never considered. Others put limits on their willingness to hear and change. Their shallow spirit is incapable of opening up to the richness of the saving word. When it begins to sprout, to make demands, they cannot commit themselves to nourishing it.

Other hearers are capable and resourceful but scattered and uncommitted to the challenges of the word of God in their lives. They can see its beauty, but they allow their hearts to attach themselves to many other attractions in life. So they try to compromise, to serve God and Mammon. In their lack of commitment to the demands of the word, they choke it. This is another way of not hearing.

Ongoing Demands of the Kingdom of God

Only those coming to the parables with a depth of personal faith provide adequate soil for the word to grow. For when God's word finds a reception in the human heart, it becomes more and more demanding. It wants to take possession of the whole person. The word takes over and wants to produce a hundredfold growth, in contrast to the sevenfold growth of a fertile natural harvest.

To become a disciple of Jesus one must give all. The seed demands all one's effort. The parable of the sower is a striking illustration of the truth that only the one who loses life for Jesus and the gospel finds it (Mark 8:35). In some way all parables lead hearers or readers to embrace that profound truth. We do not really hear them except in our decision to respond to them.

The intimate exchange between seed and soil serves as an appropriate symbol of the nature of every parable as religious dialogue. It is carried on not on the surface of the soul but only in total obedience to God's all-embracing claims.

Jesus affirms God's claims in a whole spectrum of insights communicated in his parables. Their implications cover the whole range of human response. In the preaching of Jesus the image of the kingdom of God serves as symbol for both the demands and the possibilities implicit in the full response of faith.

In the Synoptics the drama of the sower is not called a parable of the kingdom, but it sheds light on what is involved in accepting it. On the one hand, it means living in an end-time horizon in all one's thoughts and activities because of faith in the reality of the kingdom. This faith knows that human destiny is not measured by goals of human making but by one's share in God's eternal plan. On the other hand, the kingdom demands mature personal responsibility.

The choice of the kingdom is made by being converted to its values every day. Matthew's treatment of the parables stresses the ethical demands most frequently. So we now turn to consider this grouping of the parables of the kingdom.

Parables of the Kingdom in Matthew (13:24-52)

The related group of expressions translated as "the kingdom [reign/rule] of God [heaven, the Father, the Son]" appears in the Synoptic Gospels eighty-six times. These phrases never appear in the Hebrew Bible, although the idea of God as king was common among Jews. The announcement that the kingdom has arrived is a summary of the revelation of Jesus (Matt 4:17).

The kingdom of God is a reality beyond both the comprehension and the accomplishment of mortals by their own powers. In a word, it is a mystery in the religious sense of an inexhaustible truth. Parables point the way to this mystery and invite hearers to celebrate it in faith.

At times, Christians seem to identify the kingdom with the Church. The two are related but not identical. Matthew, the author of the Church Gospel, gives the most parables about the kingdom, ten in all. He groups six of them near the center of his Gospel in his great parable discourse. Up to that point he had not recorded any narrative parables of Jesus.

By bringing a whole series of these kingdom parables together, Matthew is able to communicate the complexity of the message of Jesus, which evolved over a period of time. This concentration gives special prominence to the kingdom and invites readers to embrace the new age. They are made more aware of the paradoxes involved in their choice.

On a deeper level the parables show believers that it is not they who choose the kingdom. The grace and power of God chooses and attracts them like the pearl of great price. It makes all their sacrifices to enter worthwhile (13:45-46). The parables are speech acts granting believers the keys to enter the kingdom of God. They translate the universal saving mission of Jesus into striking concrete images.

To "hear" or accept the parable is to experience the power of Jesus at work in images that transform one's world like the leaven transforms the dough (13:33). Jesus saw that many would not risk all to accept the kingdom of God. At times the dragnet of his preaching caught very few fish, and even some of these had to be let go (47-49).

At the end of this sermon on the parables of the kingdom, Matthew pictures Jesus as turning to his disciples. He asks them if they have understood his revelation. When they respond with a confident yes, he reminds them that they are being given the responsible task of being overseers of the kingdom. They must make available to others things new and old, the riches of the wisdom of the kingdom (52).

These parables show that for Jesus, the kingdom was an experienced reality. It was already bursting upon him, imposing and directing his mission. After his death the kingdom was identified with Jesus by the apostles. The parables then became Jesus' revelation to the Church. They continue to make his presence, his power, and his mystery available to believers. By preserving these images, Matthew helps the Church keep alive its end-time faith that Jesus will return as Bridegroom.

In the final parable of the kingdom of God (25:1-13), Matthew nourishes a spirit of watchfulness and hope for the return of Jesus. He tells the story of the ten virgins of the wedding party. Believers are to prepare themselves for the coming of their risen Lord, just as the five prudent virgins prepared themselves for the groom by keeping their lamps supplied.

Teaching by Parables in Luke (10:25-37)

By tradition Luke has been represented as a painter. Whether he painted portraits we do not know. But he certainly does paint word pictures. Along with his vivid character portrayals in parables, Luke uses them to sharpen the image of Jesus as hero and model of action. As wise teacher sent by God, the Jesus of Luke's Gospel creates minidramas capable of inspiring converts from paganism to embrace the vigorous life of faith.

To give his parables greater impact and appeal, Luke carefully places them throughout his Gospel. He frames them by significant scenes that highlight their message.

A good example is his way of dealing with the lawyer's question about conditions necessary to gain eternal life. In the Gospels of both Matthew and Mark this question occurs during the controversies leading up to the betrayal of Jesus in Jerusalem. Jesus, as interpreter of the Law, answers it briefly. God demands that we love him and one another.

Luke makes two important modifications. First, he switches the place of the question into the narrative of Jesus' journey to Jerusalem. Second, into this frame he inserts the parable of the Good Samaritan. The love that fulfills God's law does good to others without placing any restrictions. The lawyer was looking for certain qualifications within others that would make them worthy of his going out to them in love (Luke 10:25-37).

Jesus rejects this approach and insists that a believer's love be universal and spontaneous. It imitates God's compassion toward all. In this parable Jesus links two realities that his audience were not capable of joining: to be good and to be a Samaritan. Ardent hostility blinded the Jews to any good in the heretical Samaritans.

The fact that this parable has given the term "Samaritan" a favorable connotation in English often obscures its demanding teaching. But understood in its original context, this parable offers a continual challenge to Christian readers. It forces them to see themselves as the beggar in the ditch, helpless and in need of God's compassion in Jesus in order to be nursed back to life. It is a vivid call to imitate the total generosity of love, "Go and do likewise" (Luke 10:37).

The Difficult Parable of Luke (16:1-7)

Luke avoids stringing parables together as Matthew does in his great sermon on the kingdom. Luke's style is to present each parable as a distinct and carefully created discourse, often in connection with the teaching of Jesus on one particular quality of living. He prefers to designate the audience addressed and to round out the passage with a few wisdom sayings of Jesus so that the two types of language clarify each other and form a clear unity.

A good example of this method is found in the way Luke presents the difficult parable of the evil manager (16:1-7). The antihero has been enriching himself instead of his employer, an absentee landowner. As the parable opens he has just been exposed! What can he do to provide for his future?

This crisis galvanizes the manager into his first creative action in many years. In the short period while he still has control of the records, he manages to insure his personal future. He quickly calls in his employer's debtors and cuts deals with them to reduce their debts. His response to the crisis is to make sure that he is taken care of. The parable ends with the description of his clever maneuver to create a new set of books.

The reader is caught off-guard. But that is the nature of parables, to be open ended. What it reveals is not complete until it evokes a response from the reader. Each is forced to ask, How am I coming to terms with my destiny? Life is short. If we put off assuming responsibility, we are lost.

But what about the manager's unscrupulous way of providing for his future? The antihero's conduct obviously caused problems for Christian preachers. As they told the parable, they applied it to other situations. Luke has collected several of their practical sayings and placed them at the end of this provocative parable. The end-time parable of Jesus now serves as an entrée into a series of moral exhortations (16:8-13).

Parables and Discipleship

The revelation of the mystery of the kingdom in parables is never finished. They remain on the cutting edge of Christian preaching as it confronts each new generation. Each audience will hear them in a slightly different way because of culture, background, and experience. Only by thoughtful hearing can modern readers find the means of converting these choice fruits of the creativity of Jesus into the poetry of God's healing for modern banality.

Revelation is for serving. Jesus reminded the Pharisees, "The good person makes good things available from a good treasure" (Matt 12:35). The power of parables is to open up new forms of prayerful dialogue with the heart of Jesus. The presence of his Spirit enables believers to meet new challenges facing them in a secular world. Since each person confronts unique problems, parables will not say the same thing to each one. Yet they still build bridges from the incarnate Word to every people in every age. From the hope they give, the Church can say, "Thy kingdom come!"

FOLLOW UP

A danger exists in taking too narrow an approach to studying the parables. We want to know what a parable means, and we turn to a commentary to get "the" answer. But parables are metaphors that operate on a variety of levels. A better follow-up to this chapter would be to learn more about the world and language of Jesus. An incisive look at his imaginative language and especially his use of "focal instance" is Robert C. Tannehill, *The Sword of His Mouth* (Philadelphia: Fortress, 1975).

Important studies on parable language are collected in Amos N. Wilder, *Jesus' Parables and the War of Myths* (Philadelphia: Fortress, 1982). With that background readers will profit by Bernard Brandon Scott, *Hear Then the Parable* (Minneapolis: Fortress, 1989).

7

Luke Offers the Good News to Gentiles

The call of Saul of Tarsus to faith in Jesus was one of the turning points in the early Church's growth. By background he was a Pharisee. He wrote that he had been so zealous for the Law of Moses that he persecuted the followers of Jesus. His conversion, commemorated in his change of name to Paul, brought about a crucial change in his attitude toward the Law. He recognized that it could not bring salvation.

Paul spent his Christian missionary career sharing his new insight. His approach brought him into conflict not only with believing Jews but with many Christian Jews as well. They wished to maintain customs from the Mosaic Law. Paul vehemently opposed that approach. Christ broke down all barriers between human beings and created one new body, the Church.

One of the followers and companions of Paul was Luke. Paul calls him a "co-worker" (Phlm 24). Second Timothy, a kind of last will and testimony of Paul, states that only Luke was with the imprisoned Paul (4:11). Whether the Luke to whom the third Gospel is attributed was this disciple of Paul is not certain, but tradition identifies them, and I follow that point of view in this chapter.

Witness to Paul's Work

Luke himself tells his readers that he was not a companion of the earthly Jesus. He depends on "eyewitnesses and ministers of the word" (Luke 1:2) for accuracy, and his theology obviously reflects the preaching of Paul. Paul evidently died before Luke wrote his Gospel, because he dedicates his work to Theophilus (friend of God), perhaps a patron.

It may seem strange that Luke should write a Gospel. He was not an apostle and probably not even a Jew. Yet he had special qualifications for assuming this role. As Paul's disciple, he learned "the word of the cross" from missionary experience. He saw the saving power of the good news bring healing to believers and endow them with every form of spiritual gift.

Luke experienced the flexibility of the gospel message. It brought good news to all types of people in every level of society. His background made him sensitive to the needs of converts from paganism. He knew the kind of encouragement they needed to undertake a life-style more demanding than the permissive moral standards of the Hellenistic world.

In addition, from his study of Greek philosophy, history, and literature, Luke knew how pagans developed codes of personal ethics. Homer was still the textbook in the schools attended by young aristocrats. Society at large learned standards of conduct from the great tragedies performed at annual festivals.

These festivals had both religious and patriotic dimensions. The character flaws of the tragic heroes aroused an emotional purification in the spectators. The theory of tragedy was that this purging (*katharsis*) would lead to a more noble life.

Closer to the time of Jesus, another educational tool was available in the "kingship tracts," often written for princes. These were ethical guides for those destined to become rulers of Hellenistic cities. They set up moral standards for personal integrity, social responsibility, and political maturity. They were widely read by ambitious civic leaders who wanted to win friends and influence people.

The audience Luke addressed needed to see Jesus in terms of its cultural ideals as a moral hero who could be respected and worshiped. Without such an example, these converts from Hellenistic philosophy or popular mystery cults would find difficulty in sustaining the high ideals of their new Christian faith. Once they were convinced that Jesus was alive and still present in the world and interested in their salvation, they would respond to the challenges his Church offered.

Luke did not make the mistake of equating Jesus with other popular religious heroes. His Gospel enters into dialogue with Greek culture but maintains a tension between divine revelation and human reason. If he seems to compare Jesus to Greek heroes, he also distinguishes them.

Jesus is Lord in a unique, transcendent manner. He is God's Son. As a result, believers are both liberated and enslaved by him. Jesus is more powerful and more compassionate than humans can imagine. At the same time, his demands are also farther reaching than any human power can impose.

Luke Modifies the Gospel Genre

Like the other evangelists, Luke writes as representative of the apostolic Church. His task is not to change tradition but to adapt it to the changing needs of ever-expanding groups of Christians. His primary audience consisted of cultured Greek-speaking converts to Christianity who knew no Hebrew. They had little interest in the niceties of Jewish Law and customs. They were taking their new faith into distant lands and needed to deal with the expectations of diverse cultures.

Luke accepts the basic direction that the Gospel of Mark created as a new literary form. His modifications are not drastic enough to create a distinct form of literature. Like that of Mark, Luke's Gospel is a revelation, inviting prayerful reflection and active response from readers.

By reflecting upon Luke's macrorhetoric and microrhetoric, believers arrive at a personal appreciation of the person and mission of Jesus. Four of the principal objectives evident in the Gospel of Luke are as follows:

1. To exalt the person of Jesus, Son and Messiah of God. This goal is evident in Luke's infancy narrative. Jesus appears as "great," as "Son of the Most High," and as king of Israel (1:32). When his mother visits her cousin Elizabeth, she is greeted as "the mother of my Lord" (1:43).

Luke continues to feature the title "Lord" for Jesus. His disciples address him by this title on a regular basis. Readers are to understand this title in the full postresurrection meaning: Jesus is living, universal ruler of heaven and earth. He is more than another Hellenistic benefactor.

2. To present the Holy Spirit as guiding the earthly Jesus. Luke uses the expression "Holy Spirit" more frequently than the other evangelists. He comes upon Mary to bring about the conception of Jesus (1:35). The baptism of Jesus is accompanied by a descent of the Holy Spirit. Then Jesus, filled with the Spirit, is led into the desert to undergo temptation (4:1). Jesus rejoices in the Holy Spirit when he sees his disciples driving out unclean spirits (10:21).

3. To show that the followers of Jesus are his "slaves." The word is to be understood in the religious sense found of heroes of the Hebrew Scriptures. "The slave of the Lord" is one who responds to God's call with total dedication. When the angel tells Mary her predestined role as mother of Jesus, she responds, "Behold the Lord's slave girl" (1:37). In her song of praise before Elizabeth, Mary thanks God for looking upon the lowliness of his "slave girl" (1:48).

Mary's generous response to God's favor corresponds to what Luke observed throughout the life of Paul. He too saw himself as slave of the Lord Jesus. And when the aged Simeon took Jesus into his arms and recognized him as God's gift of salvation, he identified himself as the Lord's slave (2:29).

Jesus urges his followers to cultivate that attitude of total dedication in the parable of the slave returning late from working in the fields. After exerting himself all day, he still has to get his master's supper and thinks nothing of it. No human can put God under obligation, for "we are all useless slaves" (17:10).

4. To show the saving power of faith. Luke records four occasions when Jesus tells the people he cured, "Your faith has saved you" (7:50; 8:48; 17:19; 18:42). The faith of the tax collector Zacchaeus draws Jesus into his home. Only by faith do we benefit from the mission of the Son of Man, who came "to seek and save what was lost" (19:10).

Luke's Infancy Gospel (1:5–2:52)

Like Matthew, Luke inserts an infancy gospel before his account of the public ministry of Jesus. It presents the coming of Jesus as fulfilling the messianic longings of the Jews by constantly alluding to persons, events, and themes of the Hebrew Scriptures. Luke's method of communicating his theological insights is the use of allusion; he never quotes Jewish Scripture directly in this part of his Gospel. He agrees with Matthew on key features of the story of the infancy of Jesus—that Jesus sprang from the line of King David and was born of a virgin mother in the city of Bethlehem during the reign of King Herod the Great. However, Luke's infancy gospel is three times as long as that of Matthew and is filled with poetic language and images. Its style evokes gratitude and praise for God's favor to those who trust in the fulfillment of God's promises. The infancy gospel of Luke is constructed in a series of seven scenes, a symbolic number of fullness.

These seven scenes act as a hinge between God's promises to Israel and their fulfillment in the mission of Jesus. On the one side, they link Jesus to John the Baptizer and the messianic hopes nourished by the prophets. On the other side, they proclaim the absolute superiority of Jesus and prepare readers to honor him as both the glory of his people Israel and Savior of all the nations.

The mission of Jesus is to the lowly. He will be recognized and accepted only by those who, like Mary, are persons of faith and humility. "Behold the slave girl of the Lord, be it done to me according to your word" (1:38). The power of faith is confirmed by the greeting of Elizabeth. She calls Mary "blessed" not only because she is "mother of my Lord" but also because the Lord's promises will be accomplished in her (1:43-45). Mary as a woman of faith is already blessed as an active participant in God's saving work in Jesus.

The seven scenes of Luke's infancy gospel form two sets of weighted diptychs, that is, parallel pictures, but arranged to emphasize the events in which Jesus was involved. The first set describes the birth announcements of John and Jesus. It is weighted in favor of Jesus by the addition of the scene of Mary's visit to Elizabeth. She proclaims Jesus as Lord although he is still in Mary's womb. Mary responds with the *Magnificat*, a song celebrating God's favor and mercy toward the poor as fulfilling his promises to Abraham.

The second set of parallel scenes describes the birth and circumcision of John and Jesus. Zechariah, John's unbelieving father, is freed from his muteness and recites a double blessing to praise God and his son, John. Zechariah blesses God for sending the Messiah to ransom his people. He also blesses John as a prophet sent to bring light and peace to the chosen people. Luke portrays Jesus as born in a manger in David's city of Bethlehem and announced to shepherds by angels. The scene adding weight to Jesus describes his presentation in the Temple. There he is greeted by the pious Simeon as "light of revelation to the Gentiles and glory of [God's] people Israel" (2:32).

Luke constructs a seventh scene to form the narrative climax to the infancy gospel, namely, the finding of Jesus in the Temple. During the annual pilgrimage to Jerusalem when Jesus is twelve years old, he remains in the Temple after Mary and Joseph have started back home. They come back to find him, only to be greeted by the mysterious words that he has to devote himself to the affairs of his Father (2:49). That affirmation points to the revelatory nature of the infancy gospel. Its goal is to proclaim the person of Jesus. His dignity as hero comes from his divine origin and mission. Luke invites readers to join with Mary in reflecting in their hearts on the events that God is bringing about for our salvation through Jesus (2:51).

In brief, then, a double theological message permeates Luke's infancy gospel:

1. *The primacy of salvation history.* God's overarching plan for human salvation is coming to its fulfillment in the mission of Jesus.

2. *Paschal Christology.* Even before his birth, Jesus was chosen by the Father through the overshadowing action of the Holy Spirit to communicate the salvation that God has prepared for all peoples. This theological thrust gives Luke's infancy account its nature as "gospel." It is already a challenge to readers to join the lot of the lowly by entrusting their persons and lives to the all-caring Father. Reading a gospel is a decision of faith. The good

news embodies the response of surrender to Jesus and God's Son and our Savior.

The Messianic Program of Jesus (4:16-30)

After Jesus is baptized by John and commissioned for his mission by the heavenly voice, he goes into the desert to face temptation by the devil (4:1-13). There he shows himself as God's loyal Son. Next he is led "by the power of the Spirit into Galilee" (4:14).

At this point Luke creates with masterful rhetorical skill a programmatic scene to summarize the whole ministry of Jesus. This scene foreshadows the mission and fate of Jesus in a way similar to Greek tragedies, which were familiar to Luke's readers. Greek tragedies invited audience participation by having the opening chorus summarize the plot. The goal was to enable the audience to identify with the hero and thus experience a catharsis that cleansed their characters.

This programmatic scene unfolds in the synagogue of the town where Jesus was reared. As the scene opens, he is welcomed as a visiting rabbi and invited to deliver the commentary on the Scripture reading of the day. Luke records the reading as a composite text combining Isaiah 61:2-3 and 58:6. It describes the prophet's anointing by the Spirit to preach a "jubilee" to the blind and the oppressed. A biblical jubilee came about every fifty years. It was the time of restoration of the territory given by God to the tribes of Israel in the Holy Land (see Lev 25:10).

Jesus affirms that the promised divine goal of restoration is being carried out at this very moment in special messianic fulfillment. The model for Jesus' preaching here is Luke's theology of salvation history, which underlies his "orderly account" (1:3). The mission of Jesus is the fulfillment of God's promises and plan of salvation. Jesus illustrates that the fulfillment will be the topic of the entire Gospel, summarized here in three stages:

Stage 1 (4:16-22a, anticipating 4:31-9:50). This is the period when the preaching of Jesus will meet with great success and will inspire wonder and enthusiasm among Galilean hearers.

Stage 2 (4:22b-27, anticipating 9:51-18:14). This is the period of transition, symbolized in the journey. Jesus will encounter some hesitation and resistance on the part of his hearers. People will question his motives and challenge his sincerity. In turn, Jesus will respond with his own challenges in the vivid and provocative parables on his great "journey" to Jerusalem.

Stage 3 (4:28-30, anticipating 18:15-24:53). The anger aroused by the universalism of Jesus and the unsuccessful attempt of people in his native city to put him to death foreshadow the time when he will be betrayed by his own people and be turned over to the Romans to be put to death. At that moment the Father will snatch Jesus from his enemies and give him glory.

In employing this dramatic rhetorical technique at the start of the mission of Jesus, Luke involves his readers in the events Jesus will undergo—their participation in the story involves them in the drama of salvation history. They too must make the decision whether to accept or reject Jesus as their Savior.

After fleeing his hometown, Jesus sets up headquarters for proclaiming the kingdom of God by word and deed in the Galilean city of Capernaum. Keeping to his plan for an "orderly account," Luke pictures Jesus as performing a miraculous catch of fish (5:8-11) before calling and attracting his first disciples. That miracle provides their motivation for leaving everything to follow Jesus.

The Sermon on the Plain
and Galilean Preaching (6:20-9:50)

Only after Jesus has visited many cities and cured the sick does he select his special disciples who are to work closely with him. Immediately he instructs them in a Lukan variation of the great Galilean sermon. But it takes place not on the mountain (which symbolizes for Luke the place of prayer, the place to speak to God) but on the plain (symbol of interpersonal sharing among humans). Jesus prepares for this new step in his mission by spending the whole night in prayer (6:12-15).

The brevity and tight structure of the Sermon on the Plain illustrates that Luke continues to use rhetorical tools in presenting the preaching of Jesus. His method differs significantly from the style of Matthew. Luke keeps his sermons brief. He regularly pictures Jesus as delivering short sermons devoted to one specific topic.

Luke structures this Sermon on the Plain with an eye for balance, a feature that shows Hellenistic influence on his Gospel. Jesus opens not with a set of Beatitudes only. Rather, he balances four Beatitudes with four woes, or prophetic laments. The rest of the Sermon on the Plain is structured symmetrically around the theme of imitating God as "compassionate" (6:36).

That central ideal of compassion is articulated in a series of developments. The sermon offers principles and examples about conduct toward both enemies and fellow community members. The short development concludes with the same type of appeal to fruitful conduct found at the end of Matthew's Sermon on the Mount. However, Luke's building imagery adopts the features of city dwellings with substantial foundations. This brief comparison between these two sermons illustrates that each evangelist was a true author who packaged traditional materials creatively to make the greatest impact and appeal for intended audiences.

One third of this short version is not in Matthew's very long Sermon on the Mount. At the same time, Luke incorporates pieces of advice found in other contexts in Matthew. Thus, Luke skillfully turns this opening sermon of Jesus into a plea for universal love, the foundation of all Christian ethics. His Sermon on the Plain offers readers who lack the highly developed moral code of Judaism a challenging program of interpersonal relations (6:20-49).

Luke's picture of the Galilean ministry of Jesus is similar to that narrated in the Gospels of Mark and Matthew. But he also adapts it to the needs of his Gentile audience by adding scenes that offer them encouragement. The raising to life of the only son of the widow of Naim illustrates the compassion of Jesus for the helpless (7:11-17). The scene of the repentant woman washing the feet of Jesus proclaims that faith opens salvation to everyone of good will (7:36-50). Luke notes that the disciples of Jesus included generous women who supported Jesus out of their resources (8:1-3).

To provide room for the journey narrative, Luke shortens the Galilean ministry of Jesus by omitting the last part of Mark's third cycle (cf. Mark 6:45–8:26). Perhaps the most striking difference

is Luke's omission of one of the stories of the multiplication of
the loaves.

Jesus Journeys Toward Jerusalem (9:51–18:14)

The most striking literary feature of the ministry of Jesus unique
to Luke is this "great addition," cast in the form of a journey.
This is a famous literary technique, as old as Homer's *Odyssey*.
Jesus undertakes this voyage to the Holy City with the zeal of
a biblical prophet. When the people of Galilee prove irrespon-
sive to the call to the kingdom, Jesus fixes his eyes upon Jerusalem with determination to take his mission to the highest
officials of Judaism (9:51).

The long journey narrative that begins with that stance of Jesus
is not an actual itinerary but rather a rhetorical masterpiece. It
is artistically composed to reveal the person of Jesus to a cosmopolitan audience. Some of Luke's most famous parables appear in it.

Near the start of the journey, Jesus sends out seventy-two disciples in pairs to every town or locality he intends to visit to announce the kingdom of God (10:1-12). This symbolic incident
provides a basis for recognizing the universal missionary task of
the Christian community to every nation. The joyful return of
these disciples serves as the occasion for Jesus to exult in the Holy
Spirit and to praise his Father for making the revelation of universal salvation available to the little ones of the world (10:21-24).

In the controversy with the lawyer that immediately follows,
Jesus narrates the parable of the Good Samaritan to illustrate the
universality of the biblical command to love all persons as neighbors (10:29-37). Then, faithful to his love for balance, Luke immediately inserts an insight into love by means of the visit of Jesus
to the home of Mary and Martha. Martha seems to have grasped
the meaning of love of neighbor when she calls upon Jesus to affirm her in her understanding of hospitality. But Jesus uncovers
a deeper dimension of love when he affirms Mary's listening to
the word of God as a good that all persons can claim by right
(10:38-42). Prayer is an expression of love that balances and in-
spires action.

This journey section reinforces the tradition of Luke as a
painter, an artist who constructs vivid pictures of Jesus as God's

Messiah and Savior. The entire journey is an expressive picture of Jesus as faithful prophet, determined to bear witness to his mission in the Holy City that kills the prophets God sends to call it to conversion (13:22-35).

Jesus will not refuse his date with destiny. Yet his goal is not the earthly city but the "ascension," the word Luke carefully chooses to describe the journey by which Jesus travels through his sufferings to the Father in obedience (9:51). Two unforgettable parables, carrying urgent messages, bring the Gospel of Luke back to parallel development with Matthew and Mark. The first is the story of the widow and the unjust judge. Luke tells readers that Jesus spoke this parable to teach the need "of praying always and not giving up" (18:1). The second, the parable of the Pharisee and the tax collector, comes as a warning to those who were "trusting in themselves and despising others" (18:9).

Themes Characteristic of Luke's Gospel

Luke recognized that the Good News encountered special problems in taking root in the cosmopolitan society of the Roman Empire. So he carefully tailors his presentation of the revealing words and deeds of Jesus to the special needs of his audience. This concern accounts for special features both in form and in content. For example, Luke makes use of the setting of a banquet for the parables of Jesus (14:1-24). This setting recalls the literary technique of the symposium, a gathering enabling Jesus to communicate his wisdom.

The tendency to place too much reliance on personal ability was particularly common for members of Luke's audience. He wrote to self-reliant Hellenists skilled in the practical wisdom of Roman cities. They could easily think that their insights created the future. Against this self-assurance, Luke retains the saying of Jesus that "the kingdom of God does not come with observation," that is, as subject to human investigation (17:20). God is not subject to human control.

Believers freely move beyond earthly preoccupations because of the power of Christ's intimate presence through his Spirit. The effect of his resurrection is already at work in the community. The lordship of Jesus in glory is what brings believers to salvation. Luke's Gospel calls attention to this power because the delay of the return of Jesus was troubling some members of the Church. They were disappointed at the extended delay and were becoming discouraged.

Luke indicates that the risen Jesus is already present. He shows this by moving part of the great apocalyptic discourse of Jesus into the advice he gives to his disciples on their way to Jerusalem (17:22-37). What people do each day, how they respond to the activity of the Spirit, decides their final fate. The punishments of God at the time of Noah and Lot serve as illustrations and warnings to believers today.

To help his readers combat discouragement, Luke pictures Jesus as constantly renewing himself by prayer. He spends the whole night praying before making the choice of the twelve apostles (5:12-13). His disciples observe that life of prayer, and one of them asks how they can enjoy a similar experience. Jesus responds with a personal version of the Lord's Prayer. Luke rounds out this picture of prayer by placing here the parable of the friend who comes begging for food at midnight and by adding the assurances that Jesus gives about God's desire that believers persevere in prayer (11:1-13).

On another occasion, when a man tries to get Jesus to persuade his brother to share their inheritance, Jesus warns against greed. It is in this context that Luke locates the parable about the rich farmer who tears down his barns to build bigger ones. Jesus spells out the lesson of that parable by adding reflections on confidence in God (12:13-34).

Prayer and confidence lead to the spiritual childhood that Jesus recommends (18:17). By contrast, to place one's trust in things that are passing and unable to be saved is to cut one's life off from God, who alone can save.

No wonder the disciples cry out one day, "Increase our faith!" Jesus says they need faith only the size of a mustard seed. Its built-in dynamism effects marvels (17:5-6). This saying of Jesus is a warning against looking on God's gifts as our own accomplishment—a real danger for zealous disciples. The power of faith becomes so much a part of them that they are tempted to think of it as a personal accomplishment.

In a society that contained large numbers of oppressed and alienated groups, Luke presents Jesus as not only declaring that the hungry, the mourners, the persecuted, and the peacemakers are blessed by God (6:21-22) but that in Jesus, God actively reaches out to them. He raises the only son of the widow of Naim (7:11-15) and heals a crippled woman on the Sabbath in spite of opposition from the Jewish establishment (13:10-17).

In befriending a prominent tax collector, Zacchaeus, Jesus affirms his openness toward sinners. "The Son of Man came to seek out and save what was lost" (19:10). By conducting an active ministry among the lowly, Jesus proclaims that he is imitating God, who is "kindly toward the ungrateful and evil" (6:35). Not that Jesus is indulgent toward his followers. On the contrary, those who wish to become his followers must "hate" every member of their own family, and say "no" to their own lives.

To be a disciple of Jesus is like building a tower: Unless the foundation is dug deep, the project will collapse (14:25-30). How are modern readers to understand this radical cost of discipleship? Jesus insists that believers cannot live a shallow existence. They are challenged to transcend the selfish interests of this world with its preoccupations. When they have responded to all the demands of taking up their cross every day, they still acknowledge, "We are unprofitable slaves; we have done what we were called to do" (17:10).

Living in the New Age

Our rapid survey of the Gospel of Luke is sufficient to show that Luke wants to demonstrate to his readers that they are living in the new age, the final stage in salvation history, the eschatological period when "the kingdom of God is in our midst" (17:21). He does not direct their attention to the glorious return of Jesus as Son of Man coming on clouds of glory. Rather, he celebrates the whole of this period. He exhorts the disciples of Jesus in the Roman Empire to live each day with their cross, to stand prepared to render an account of their stewardship "like people expecting their master." They should be ready to welcome the Lord Jesus at all times and places in the magnificent variety of human beings (12:35-48).

Believers in this new age pray "each day" for necessary food and for power to resist temptations (11:3). To keep them mindful of their status, Luke directs toward them some aspects of the apocalyptic sermon that Matthew and Mark record immediately before the passion as addressed only to disciples of Jesus. As I stated above, Luke incorporates certain aspects into an earlier discussion between Jesus and a Pharisee (17:20-37). He also pictures Jesus as being more open about the great cosmic conflict by having him deliver the apocalyptic sermon itself publicly in the Temple (21:5).

By the way he describes the destruction of Jerusalem, Luke recalls to his readers the intense sufferings resulting from the fall of Jerusalem in 70 c.e., possibly ten years before he put this Gospel together. He encourages them to remain faithful in the face of the continuing persecutions. Jesus promised, "A hair of your head will not be lost; in your patience you will possess your lives" (21:19). Their faithful suffering is the "beginning of redemption" (21:28).

In the interpretation of Luke, the final warning of Jesus to his followers is that they keep guard over their actions so that they will not fall under the domination of sin. Only if they "keep watch at every moment," will they escape ever-present danger and arrive safe and secure before the Son of Man (21:34-36).

A sense of commitment is essential for Christians living in the midst of this generation. As model of total dedication, Jesus invites them to imitate the simplicity of a child: "Whoever does not receive the kingdom of God like a child will not enter into it" (18:17).

FOLLOW UP

Its frequent use of Jesus as a model of conduct makes the Gospel of Luke attractive to readers looking for guidance. Many inspiring commentaries on it are available. Charles H. Talbert, *Reading Luke* (New York: Crossroad, 1982) does not cover every passage but emphasizes the themes of Jesus fulfilling prophecy, displaying divine power by his mighty deeds, and serving as the model hero for believers.

J. Massyngbaerde Ford, *My Enemy is My Guest* (Maryknoll: Orbis, 1984) offers Luke's portrait of the nonviolent Jesus as especially appropriate for Christians living in the most violent age of the world. In *The Narrative Unity of Luke-Acts: A Literary Interpretation*, Volume 1: *The Gospel of Luke* (Philadelphia: Fortress, 1986), Robert C. Tannehill makes a special effort to understand the characters in terms of their unfolding role in the plot of the Gospel.

8

Miracles: Signs of the Kingdom at Work

Jesus makes the power of the kingdom of God available to believers not only by parables but also by his mighty deeds, which we commonly call miracles today. These two forms of revelation go hand in hand. A miracle is a parable in action, just as parables are miracles in speech. Neither is possible without faith, because belief is the context in which God brings the saving presence of his kingdom into human history.

Mark notes that when Jesus returned to his hometown of Nazareth early in his public ministry, "he could not perform any mighty deeds there" because the inhabitants did not have any faith in him (Mark 6:5-6). They refused to see God at work in and through Jesus. From the biblical perspective, miracles do not work outside of the believer's expectations. They assume the personal involvement of God at every level of creation. They are not pieces of magic to dazzle skeptics or to force assent from unwilling spectators.

In this sense, then, miracles are an essential element of gospel truth. Modern readers can understand them only by studying how they function within the gospel text. This chapter investigates how the mighty deeds of Jesus are portrayed in the Synoptic Gospels.

In the Gospels, the mighty deeds of Jesus form part of the cultural and literary "universe of discourse" of the early Christian community. Culturally, they are an integral feature of that religious society that was created and sustained by the Lord, the God of heaven and earth (the Hebrew way of designating the universe).

They are signs that God is still at work in his creation, guiding it to its destiny by his powerful presence. The Bible accepts all reality as subject to God. His wisdom and power constantly shape human existence.

In terms of their literary universe of discourse, the Synoptic Gospels describe miracles in a simple narrative form. That form, or genre, has three parts, namely, (1) a description of a need or problem; (2) the intervention of Jesus to resolve the difficulty, usually at the request of an interested party; and (3) some confirmation that God's power brought about the change through Jesus. This may be in the form of a positive display of wonder and praise or a negative reaction of enemies accusing Jesus of working with the devil.

At times this simple narrative genre of miracle story may be expanded to include other literary elements like polemics. Polemics feature in the story of Jesus driving demons out of a flock of pigs in Gadara (Matt 8:29-34; Mark 5:1-20; Luke 8:26-39). Early Christian preachers also developed apologetic motifs as they related the mighty deeds of Jesus to convert outsiders. These apologetic features are often incorporated into the gospel accounts of miracles.

The stories of mighty deeds were not a new literary form in New Testament times. They appear in Jewish Scriptures, especially in Exodus, when God raised up Moses to lead the Israelites out of the slavery of Egypt. They were also part of the ministry of the early prophets Elijah and Elisha, as narrated in 1 Kings 17–2 Kings 9. The same spirit of faith that enabled the Israelites to respond to the mighty deeds of Moses empowered the followers of Jesus to recognize God working through his signs and wonders.

The close link between miracles and parables is evident in the symbolic acts of Jesus. His cursing the barren fig tree and causing it to wither symbolized the fruitless condition of the chosen people at the time (Matt 21:18-21; Mark 11:12-14). Believers are those who acknowledge the working of God in their lives and in history to enable them to resist temptations and to triumph over the Evil One, who resists God's rule in the world.

As an essential part of Jesus' ministry of revelation, miracles are signs that he came as Messiah to usher in the new age, the final stage of God's saving plan. They illustrate how the fullness of the power of the kingdom and the greater justice offered by Jesus are at work to overcome the forces of evil in human history.

Jesus manifested the wonder of that power by a variety of mighty deeds:

1. By transforming the human environment in some way, Jesus made God's riches available to people in need. These are the so-called nature miracles, for example, multiplying the loaves.

2. In healing human minds and bodies, Jesus communicated his divine wholeness to the sick and diseased.

3. By exorcizing humans from devils dwelling within them, Jesus liberated them from powerful demonic forces believed to be present in the world. Exorcisms feature prominently in the many summaries of the miracles of Jesus in Mark (for example, Mark 1:32-34, 39; 3:11; 6:7).

All these types of miracles are signs to reveal that the power of the Father's kingdom is now at the disposal of believers through the activity of Jesus. The way these stories are told makes it evident that miracles do not belong to the genre of scientific discourse. They are religious actions narrated according to the rules of religious language. To interpret New Testament miracles on the basis of some modern definition of miracle, like that of David Hume (a violation of the laws of nature), obscures their function as signs to reveal the kingdom of God at work.

Miracles Stirred Up Controversy

The Gospel of Mark devotes about 30 percent of its material to its eighteen miracle stories. These play an important part in the conflicts that erupt between Jesus and the Jewish authorities, which eventually lead to his death. It is worth looking at that material now.

As soon as Jesus starts to teach in the local synagogue (Jewish place of prayer) at Capernaum, an unclean spirit recognizes divine power at work and protests: "What's between us and you, Jesus of Nazareth? Have you come to destroy us? I know who you are, O Holy One of God" (Mark 1:24). The ability of Jesus to drive out this spirit is a sign that the victory of the kingdom of God over the powers of Satan has begun.

Jesus continues to display divine power by curing the mother-in-law of Peter (1:29-31) and by a whole evening spent curing the sick and exorcizing demons (1:32-34). In fact, Mark summarizes Jesus' early ministry of teaching the people of Galilee about God by describing a series of miraculous cures and exorcisms (1:39-45).

With his return to his base in Capernaum, Jesus becomes the center of controversy because of all his mighty deeds. The Jewish lawyers, called "scribes," accuse him of being a blasphemer, one who has been trying to usurp God's prerogatives (Mark 2:7). When Jesus invites a tax collector to join in his mission, the scribes and Pharisees show resentment. But Jesus insists and informs them that his mission is to heal sinners and to work signs to display God's mercy toward them (2:17).

These miraculous activities of Jesus force his opponents to pay attention to the authority he claims for pursuing his mission. More controversy erupts when he draws upon his power to cure at the service on the Sabbath, the holy day of rest (Mark 2:1-5). The Jews accuse him of breaking God's law. Jesus, in turn, becomes angry at their blindness for failing to see God's compassion working through him.

Jesus boldly affirms his authority as coming from God. "The Son of Man is master even of the Sabbath" (2:28). This style of acting prompts the Pharisees to join forces with followers of Herod to start plotting how they can bring about his death.

Mark indicates how this tension increases in the way he leads up to a miracle that only he narrates. As opposition to Jesus intensifies, he sees that he has to avoid hostile crowds. So Jesus secretly leaves Jewish territory for Sidon and the group of ten Hellenistic cities called the Decapolis. Even there his reputation is so great that people bring a man with "blocked speech" to him (Mark 7:32). Mark describes vividly how Jesus takes the man aside, puts his fingers into his unhearing ears, touches his wayward tongue with saliva, and then groans in agonizing prayer. Finally, Jesus orders the ears and tongue to "be opened." Immediately the man's speech and hearing are restored (7:31-35).

This narrative is a good example of the symbolic role that miracles play in announcing the new age that arrives through the mighty deeds of Jesus. Why? Because the word chosen by Mark for "blocked speech" appears in the Bible only once before, in Isaiah 35:6. That verse is part of a poetic description of the final days, when God will heal all creation as well as dwellers on the earth and will restore universal peace.

This summary of the mighty deeds of Jesus as described in Mark's Gospel shows that readers must approach them in the context of faith. His coming was the fulfillment of the prophetic hope that in the final stage of his plan God would bring the work of creation to perfection in a new creation. The messianic kingdom would be an outpouring of divine wisdom, power, and love. These accounts express the deep faith of the early Church in the working of God through its courageous witness in preaching the "Gospel of Jesus Christ, Son of God" (Mark 1:1).

The gospel miracles focus attention on an important dimension of divine revelation. The mighty deeds of Jesus force his hearers to take sides for or against the kingdom of God. No one can remain aloof. Those who are not for Jesus are against him; those who do not gather with him scatter the flock (Mark 9:40; Matt 12:30). No wonder that the second half of Mark's Gospel, which is directed to disciples, contains only three miracles, namely, the cure of the possessed boy (9:19, 22-24), the cure of the blind Bartimeus (10:46-52), and the withering of the fig tree (11:22-24). True disciples who have left all to follow Jesus no longer need mighty deeds to nourish their faith. They contrast sharply with outsiders who resolve not to believe.

The Miracle Section in Matthew (8:1–9:35)

Just as it systematizes the sermon material of Jesus, the Gospel of Matthew presents the miracles of Jesus in a more systematic manner than the other two Synoptics. Matthew carefully organizes the opening section of the mission of Jesus into the great Sermon on the Mount balanced by an artistic narrative of ten miraculous cures. That sermon is a comprehensive outline of the new law. The parallel miracle section provides a comprehensive display of the divine authority of Jesus that causes readers to marvel at the power of Jesus. These acts demonstrate that he comes to offer healing and salvation to all the burdened who come to him for refreshment (Matt 11:28-30).

This literary technique of presenting revelation in the form of skillfully constructed accounts of the words and deeds of Jesus is an artistic way of affirming for readers that God's mighty power to save is at work in and through him. The use of the inclusion technique, that is, repeating the notice of verse 4:23 at the end of the ten miracles of healing in 9:35, alerts readers that this section is a summary of the wisdom and power of Jesus, who brings salvation to the new age by "preaching the gospel of the kingdom and healing every disease and malady."

This imaginative method of paralleling the ethical demands of the kingdom of God in the Sermon on the Mount with the miracle section demonstrates that the lesson of the mighty deeds of Jesus goes beyond their immediate physical impact. The arrangement shows that these mighty deeds are symbols in number and kind of the divine saving power available to the readers through the Church, which Jesus enriches with his Spirit.

The number of miracles, ten, symbolizes fullness, the total availability of God's power. The range of healings symbolizes omnipotence; no need escapes divine healing. Jesus heals leprosy, fever, blindness, deafness, paralysis, hemorrhage; he even raises from the dead. Of course, he also drives out demons, which are the powerful enemies of God's kingdom.

These ten miracles make up half the miracles found in Matthew's Gospel. The impact of this concentration matches the power produced by the extended sermons found in Matthew. It proclaims the concentrated authority of God, possessed by Jesus, as now available to believers.

The series begins with the cure of the leper (8:1-4). Matthew moves this traditional healing up to first place in the narrative for a symbolic purpose. Jesus orders the cured leper to go and show himself to the Jewish priest. Then he is to make the offering prescribed in the Law of Moses as testimony that he is cured. In the Sermon on the Mount, Jesus said he came to fulfill the Law (5:17). This first miracle symbolizes that assertion. Jesus does not disregard the traditions or institutions of the chosen people. He fulfills Israel's hope of experiencing the healing presence of God in its midst.

The artificial construction of the series is also manifest in the final two cures recorded (9:27-34). To bring the list to the symbolic number of ten, these two cures are duplicates of miracles that Matthew records again in their traditional location in the Synoptic sequence. The two blind men crying out, "Have mercy on us, Son of David," appear again at the point that corresponds to the description of their cure in the Gospels of Mark and Luke, when Jesus visits Jericho on his fateful journey to Jerusalem (20:29-34). The cure of the deaf-mute occurs again when it also provokes the charge by the Pharisees that Jesus heals by the power of Beelzebul (12:24).

Miracles and Discipleship

The extended description of the ten cures by Matthew points to the existence of miracle-collections in the early Christian communities. Preachers in the apostolic Church composed brief summaries that were useful in preaching the good news. The scenes described in Matthew 8:1-18 read like the story of a day of healing in the city of Capernaum. In the evening large groups are brought to Jesus, and he cures freely. Matthew rounds out this day with one of his typical fulfillment quotations, which are explained in chapter 5.

In this quotation Matthew uses the description of the work of the Suffering Servant of the Lord from the Book of the Prophet Isaiah to express his faith in the healing ministry of Jesus. Jesus is the faithful servant who has taken upon himself the pain of God's people (8:17).

This adaptation is typical of the freedom with which the Gospel of Matthew draws on Scripture to illustrate the ministry of Jesus. The force of these appeals is to affirm that the mission of Jesus is not limited to the few months of his earthly preaching. Through the Church, the saving power of the Lord extends to all peoples, places, and ages.

The insertion of scenes about discipleship within this miracle section reinforces the symbolic name of Jesus as "Immanuel," that is, "God with us" (1:23). When would-be followers want to set limits on their commitment, Jesus responds with a parable, "Let the dead bury their own dead" (8:22). This is not a moral assessment of an individual's life-style. It is Jesus' way of stating the urgency of the new age in graphic terms. The present age is passing away. Those called to faith in the kingdom of God must not ignore this chance of salvation.

Another of the discipleship scenes in this section tells of Matthew's own call and of the banquet he offers in honor of Jesus for his tax-collector friends, who are looked down upon as sinners by the Law-abiding Pharisees. Jesus uses the occasion to teach the purpose of his revelation, namely, to call sinners to salvation. Revelation is not an abstract theory but the gift of God's wisdom and mercy, which empowers sinners in and through Jesus (9:12-13).

This creative handling of the miracles of Jesus is one way that the Gospel of Matthew imparts to readers further insight into the liberating power of the kingdom of God. The freedom it offers draws sinners into the community of believers, where the powerful presence of Jesus continues to manifest itself.

For Luke, Miracles Fortify Faith

Two features characterize the treatment of miracles in the Gospel of Luke. First, he focuses attention on the custom of Jesus to work wonders on the Sabbath, the Lord's Day of rest, as in 4:30, 33; 6:6; 13:10; 14:1. Not only does this put Jesus on a collision course with the Jewish authorities, but it also identifies his mighty deeds with the power of the Lord of the Sabbath. Miracles mirror God's will to work in and through Jesus to heal on the very day sanctified by God's law.

The second characteristic of Luke's portrayal of Jesus as miracle worker is the stress he puts on the responses that his mighty works evoke. Luke often records reactions of praise or thanks or reverent fear from people who participate in or observe these displays of divine power as, for example, in 5:25-26; 7:16; 8:35; 9:43; 13:13; 17:15; 18:43. Luke inserts such details to evoke from readers a deeper faith in God's saving presence in Jesus and to draw them into confident discipleship of the God who has brought about the transformation of the world in Jesus Christ.

The non-Jewish audience of Luke demanded from him a method of dealing with the mighty deeds of Jesus that differed from the approach of Matthew and Mark. In the prologue of his Gospel Luke promises to give readers "certainty" concerning the

events about Jesus, which has been explained in their catechetical instructions leading to baptism (1:4). In Greco-Roman culture magic was rampant. Shrines to the healing god, Asclepius,
were popular, and many miracle workers circulated in society.

What was special about Jesus as a miracle worker? Luke draws
upon cultural similarities in both positive and negative ways. On
the positive side, miracles would appeal to many Hellenistic readers. Most religious Greek readers saw miracles as proof that a
public preacher had divine backing, and they expected to see this
form of divine approval in the ministry of Jesus. On the negative
side, miracles were suspect among many educated readers of the
time. Certain philosophical schools looked on them as tricks of
magicians and would be suspicious of any preacher resorting to
them.

Awareness of this cultural situation at the time Luke was writing helps modern believers grasp the special nuances that appear
in the narratives of the twenty miracles Luke records, especially
in the six that are found only in his Gospel, namely, the miraculous catch of fish (5:1-11), raising the widow's son to life (7:11-17),
curing the woman crippled for eighteen years (13:10-17), freeing
a man from dropsy (14:2-6), curing the ten lepers (17:11-19), healing the ear of the high priest's servant (22:49-51).

Miracles Call to Discipleship in Luke (5:1-11, 27-32)

In keeping with his goal of giving an "orderly account," Luke
establishes a careful balance between the teaching and the mighty
deeds of Jesus as revealing God's kingdom at work in Jesus. Because members of his audience would have preconceptions about
miracles, both positive and negative, Luke has to exercise care
in the way he describes them. Jesus does not perform magic feats
to dazzle the crowds. His goal is to arouse repentance and to encourage trust in God.

Two vocation stories occur in the midst of the early miracles
in Luke. They point to the relation that Luke wishes to establish
between believing and discipleship. Jesus begins to preach in
Galilee and attracts large crowds. People press around him so
tightly on the shore of the lake that he asks Simon to let him use
his boat so that he can preach from it.

After preaching, Jesus tells Simon to row out farther and to throw out the nets for a catch. Simon has been preaching the whole night before and has caught nothing. Yet he obeys the request and immediately makes a huge haul of fish (5:5-7). The number is so great that Simon calls his friends in a second boat to help, but both almost sink from the load. Simon Peter (as Luke now calls him) is overcome with religious awe at this miracle and throws himself at the feet of Jesus. He is unworthy to be with a person who displays divine power. Jesus brushes aside this humble excuse and invites Peter and his companions to become sharers in God's saving work.

This same rhythm of miracle, then call to discipleship, occurs in the encounter with the tax collector Levi. Jesus is preaching and healing. A group of men bring in a paralytic but cannot get through the crowd. They go up and break through the roof and lower the man into the presence of Jesus. He forgives the man's sins. Only when the Pharisees complain does Jesus bestow physical healing. The crowd breaks forth in joy and wonder shouting, "We have seen marvels today!" (1:26).

Jesus immediately goes out and sees Levi, a tax collector, working in his office. He invites this person, so different from the Pharisees, to become his disciple with a simple "Follow me." Levi is activated by the experience of the power of Jesus and obeys immediately. This power offers him hope of salvation. It also serves as a motive for readers to trust in the care of Jesus for them. What Jesus offered to Luke's original readers was a taste of God's reaching out to them.

By including the description of similar responses to the miracles of Jesus in the story of Peter and Levi, Luke invites all types of readers to trust in God's healing power, available in Jesus. The mercy of Jesus manifests the compassion of God, which Luke holds up for our admiration and imitation (6:36). Only Luke pictures Jesus in a gesture of spontaneous compassion toward the widow who has lost her only son. Without being asked, Jesus approaches and gives him back to her alive (7:11-19).

Like the other evangelists, Luke shows that the miracles of Jesus provoke diverse responses. The cure of the ten lepers shows an interesting diversity (17:12-19). Nine of the ten simply go on their way, taking advantage of the power of Jesus to return to society.

The tenth, as soon as he senses what has happened, "returned praising God in a loud voice, and he drops to his knees in front of Jesus to thank him. And this one was a Samaritan," Luke adds with irony.

The Pharisees who observe the event take a belligerent attitude. They begin to challenge Jesus to give them signs of his legitimacy. Jesus refuses to play their game. He knows that the kingdom of God does not come "with observation," as if it could be controlled. If they truly opened their eyes, the Pharisees would see that it is already at work in their midst (17:20-21). God's power is available to those who respond with faith in Jesus.

Can Miracles Speak Today?

This survey of the Synoptic Gospels makes clear that miracles are meaningful only in the context of faith. Jesus performed them with a religious purpose in mind for people who saw reality as a whole. The evangelists portray them as part of their picture of Jesus, addressed to believers who trust that creation is the work of God and is totally subject to his wisdom and power. Believers are those who are open to divine intervention in this world and who celebrate the Providence that guides their lives toward glory.

God, who hovers over the daily needs of all, offers access through forgiveness and renewal of life in Jesus. Only those who recognize their sinfulness are able to welcome that presence and respond to the liberating power of the Lord Jesus. His miracles illustrate what he told the Pharisees who objected to the call of Levi, "I have come not to call the just but sinners to repent" (Luke 5:32).

FOLLOW UP

Most treatments of New Testament miracles as such become bogged down in apologetics. They defend details rather than focus on the reality of miracles as signs of the liberating presence of almighty God, who is more powerful than any opponent. Hence, readers do well to develop themselves in the conditions needed to appreciate the mighty deeds of Jesus as parables in action by reading about transcultural methods for the study of biblical texts.

A helpful introduction is found in Jan de Waard and Eugene A. Nida, *From One Language to Another: Functional Equivalence in Bible Translating* (Nashville: Nelson, 1986). Charles H. Kraft, *Christianity in Culture: A Study in Dynamic Biblical Theologizing in Cross-Cultural Perspective* (Maryknoll: Orbis Books, 1979), gives illustrations of how God cooperated with culturally conditioned human writers of the Bible.

9

Jesus, Servant Faithful unto Death

The first half of Mark's Gospel (1:1-8:30) portrays Jesus as the one who makes God present by words of wisdom and mighty deeds. Jesus goes forth as a "divine man," a miracle-working Messiah. He attracts a large, enthusiastic following. Yet Mark is careful not to leave readers with that image of Jesus. His real mission is to call for a change of heart, to proclaim the arrival of the kingdom of God, and to invite hearers to entrust their lives to the good news (1:15). Very soon these demands of Jesus arouse opposition, and his enemies start scheming to destroy him (3:6).

From the beginning Jesus is misunderstood not only by curious crowds but even by his followers. He has to reject Peter's proclamation of him as Messiah because it assumes a political orientation of his mission (Mark 8:32). All the Gospels show that Jesus cannot be understood within the limits of human horizons or according to the passing values of this world. God is acting in and through Jesus to reconcile the human race to himself and his destiny for them.

As the Synoptic Gospels come to their climax, it is clear that the mission of Jesus will be achieved in a paradoxical way. Jesus will be rejected precisely for his steadfast fidelity to the mission God entrusted to him. Readers are faced with the question, How could the heavenly Father expose his Son to such a situation? We are still forced to confront this question as we examine today their narratives of the rejection of Jesus and his suffering and death on the cross.

Inevitability of Confrontation

The second half of Mark's Gospel opens on the theme of the coming rejection of Jesus. He assembles his followers to prepare them for this inevitability (8:31).

Jesus makes this revelation only to his followers and not to the crowds, who show that they are unwilling to commit themselves to the values of the kingdom of God. Mark pictures Jesus as predicting his sufferings on three occasions (8:31-33; 9:30-32; 10:32-34). Even so, his disciples never grasp the tragedy of the events awaiting them. Only after his resurrection are they able to come to terms with the divinely planned destiny of Jesus. By carefully reading the Jewish Scriptures under the guidance of the Holy Spirit, they come to recognize that the Son of Man "had" to suffer and be put to death (Luke 24:26).

Why is this "had to" in Luke's Gospel? In what sense was the death of Jesus inevitable? How could he have continued in a mission through which he was being swept inexorably toward a tragic end and yet still have trusted in the God who had announced this destiny through the prophets?

The Synoptic Gospels do not attempt a psychological portrait of Jesus. They do not analyze how he grew "in wisdom and age before God and humans" (Luke 2:52). Jesus was aware of the Father's saving will and with love prepared himself to share in every prophet's rejection by his own. Yet he never deviated from the mission given him by the loving Father, who is actively present in shaping human destiny.

The sermons and parables of Jesus proclaimed that God makes the sun and rain available to good and evil alike without any distinction (Matt 5:48). Jesus knew that God wills only the good of all. From personal experience Jesus also knew that evil exists within human hearts and penetrates all structures of society. This universal permeation of evil reveals that the human race is enslaved to sin. A slavish mentality blocks God's appeal to goodness. If mortals were to be liberated from their slavery to sin, Jesus knew they must be convinced that God loves them. They must see the divine compassion come alive in God's dealings with them.

As the enemies of Jesus yielded to the destructive power of sin, his identity with the Father's will provoked them to oppose his vision of the kingdom of God. The Gospels illustrate how he saw his mission in terms of saying a loving no to sin's domination over his enemies. God asked of Jesus to turn back this tide of sin by saying no with his very life. As the earlier chapters of this book show, the Gospels as a whole do not make it possible for us to reconstruct with historical precision how Jesus actually came to this understanding.

A similar situation exists in reference to the gospel accounts of the passion. They do not give a step by step description of all the anguish of Jesus. They mirror the community's understanding of his accepting the Father's will and calling his disciples to take up their cross and follow him in the face of the alienating power of sin.

Centrality of the Passion Story

The suffering and death of Jesus cast their shadow over the last half of the ministry of Jesus in all three Synoptic Gospels. This inevitable destiny of Jesus is most clear in the way the three passion predictions dominate the second half of Mark's Gospel. These passion predictions tell readers that Jesus wanted only to respond to God's activity within him and to carry out the mission prepared for him by the Father. In that loyal response Jesus becomes model for all believers who stand against sin and selfishness to embrace the demands of the kingdom of God.

As explained in chapter 4, the minisermons that follow the three passion predictions in Mark instruct readers to take up their cross and follow Jesus. The Gospels of Matthew and Luke expand upon Mark's presentation of the ministry of Jesus, but they do not alter this radical call to become disciples of the cross. "Anyone who wishes to come after me must deny self, take up the cross and follow me" (Mark 8:34).

Jesus was conscious of being unique among humans. He was God's Son, who alone enjoyed full communion with the Father's will. Since humanity was estranged from God, this vision of Jesus "had to" confront its darkness and provoke confrontation. But reconciliation to God could not be accomplished on the surface level of abstract sermons. A much more profound message of conversion of heart was called for. Paradoxically, the revelation of God's saving love demanded the language of the cross.

Mark's repetition of the passion predictions dramatizes the inevitable conflict between God's goodness and human sinfulness. Sin blinds hearts and impels humans to reject God. When Jesus proclaimed the need of repentance for all, he provoked opposition from the righteous religious leaders of God's people. Jesus saw that he must let the torrent of sin engulf and carry him to death. That was the act destined to reconcile sinful humanity to the Father.

In obedience to this saving will of God, Jesus surrendered his desire for personal safety and escape, expressed in the prayer of his agony (Mark 14:36). He let sin exercise its power over him. The unselfishness of that act reveals the surpassing power of divine love to confront, confound, and overcome human sinfulness. Cross redemption is the act that makes divine freedom available to human hearts. The growing awareness of Jesus that he was the victim of sin did not in any sense put him at odds with the Father. God's aim in this event was not to reject and punish Jesus but to save sinners.

Jesus observed that humanity was in a fallen, slavish condition, unable to respond freely to God's offer of healing love. The very inability of the leaders of his people to accept Jesus as the suffering Messiah was a sign of the need of redemption. The overpowering act of love shown in his embracing the cross was the breakthrough that reopened channels of communication, trust, and hope in every human heart.

The Synoptic Gospels do not speculate on the self-consciousness of Jesus as he made the decision to accept his death. Their literary genre demands a narrative portrayal of God's saving activity. The evangelists show Jesus struggling with his Father's will in his agony and accepting his role as a prophet who must die in the holy city of Jerusalem (Luke 13:33). Through his obedience God restores humans to true freedom, the ability to love without selfishness.

Jesus Confronts His Opposition (Matthew 23:1-39)

More than Mark and Luke, Matthew dramatizes the growing hostility between Jesus and the Jewish authorities. They are blind to the realities of the Holy Spirit, "For they speak and do not do" (23:3). Having shown how opposition to Jesus gradually increased through his public life, Matthew now collects his attacks against the "scribes and Pharisees, hypocrites" into a series of seven "woes" or prophetic laments (23:13-29).

These outbursts decry their abuse of authority in a variety of ways. They make it hard for the poor to enter into the kingdom of God. By putting all the emphasis on showy display, they miss the important goals of God's law, "judgment and mercy and loyalty" (23:23).

In face of such blindness, Matthew shows Jesus speaking his last public words to the people in the form of a lament over the city of Jerusalem. Jesus compares his love for it to that of a mother bird. How anxious he is to gather his brood together under his maternal wings! But they refuse. They will pay a high price, the loss of their freedom (23:37-39).

Despite these harsh criticisms, Jesus still upholds the authority of the scribes and Pharisees. They hold positions on the chair of Moses; so their words are to be obeyed. At the same time Jesus is aware that his attacks will galvanize them to act against him. So it is clear that Jesus knew what he was doing. His unbending loyalty to his mission sets the opposition in motion. He knows that a clash is inevitable if he keeps to this course. And yet he continues boldly on the path that can lead only to Calvary.

Jesus' Attitude Toward His Death (Matthew 26:36-46)

This positive stance of Jesus toward those opposing him was an integral part of the "had to" of the divine plan. The Father did not decree that his Son should die unwillingly or in a purely passive way. Jesus saw violent death coming and accepted it because he loved and trusted his Father. He also felt love and compassion for fellow human beings and believed that God entrusted their salvation to his care (Matt 11:27-29).

If he was to confront and triumph over sin, Jesus had to endure the consequences of sin. When the moment of decision came upon him in the garden and his spirit shuddered at his lot in life, Jesus refused to ask his Father to intervene to prevent the struggle. He made his decision on behalf of humanity to liberate mortals from the fatal grasp of evil (Matt 26:39). The wisdom and power of God turned his death into a saving event.

Not that the Father wanted Jesus killed. But his death became inevitable in the context of humanity's alienation from God. Only God could tear down the barrier of alienation that sin had erected. The one activity capable of bringing about the reconciliation was an undeniable outpouring of unselfish love. Jesus, in perfect harmony of spirit with his Father, willingly performed that act of love.

Mark's Account of the Trial of Jesus (14:53–15:20)

Mark's account of the trial narrative brings together many themes of his Gospel. His genius as a writer appears in his ability to reconcile the paradoxes of the life of Jesus. As his model in portraying the suffering of Jesus, Mark draws upon the Jewish Scriptures, especially the traditions of the suffering just man described in Psalm 22. This he blends with the picture of the Suffering Servant of the Lord, an ideal figure painted in the Book of Isaiah to show that God's power vindicates those who trust in him (Isa 52:13–53:12).

Mark skillfully incorporates Jewish themes into his passion narrative. As a result, to understand Mark's account readers must enter into it in a spirit of faith and prayerful remembrance. Jesus suffers as the last of a long line of obedient servants sent by the Lord God to lead his people back from sin. As voice of the early community, Mark organizes these oral traditions into the unified narrative that still guides the Church in celebrating the Lord's death at the Eucharist.

Formation of the Passion Story

From the earliest preaching of the disciples of the risen Jesus, his passion and death were always preached as the central part of the "good news." They were celebrated because they were undertaken "for us and for our salvation." The story of all that Jesus endured was immediately incorporated into the apostolic preaching of salvation. That means that the passion was proclaimed with the faith conviction that Jesus had acted obediently in accord with the Father's will.

The basic passion narrative that soon developed consisted of four parts: the arrest of Jesus, his trials by Jews and Romans, the story of his crucifixion, and his resurrection, which was always an integral part of the account.

During the period of oral apostolic preaching, a variety of scenes and motifs were added to this basic outline in response to interest in details about events of the last days of Jesus and as a way of expressing concern for theological questions connected with the death of Jesus. One of these added motifs centers on questions about how Jesus fulfills passages from the prophets. At some point, the Last Supper scene was added to link the Church's Eucharistic celebrations more closely to the redemptive offering of Calvary.

Each Synoptic evangelist put material from the many oral traditions into an integrated account that would address the intended audience with impact and appeal. Jesus' appeals to his disciples to watch with him in prayer enrich the moral impact of the agony narrative. All the Synoptic accounts maintain the tension between the guiding role of tradition and the personal theological outlooks of the evangelists. A brief look at some of these scenes will show how skillfully the individual accounts carry out their function.

Mark prepares for the passion story proper by a series of vivid scenes marking the final events of the preaching of Jesus in Jerusalem. He climaxes his mission of revealing the kingdom of God by celebrating a final ritual meal with his chosen Twelve. During this meal, Jesus invokes that special blessing that would make this bread and cup the sign of the coming outpouring of his life for humanity (Mark 14:12-25). Luke alone adds the liturgical directive instructing the believing community to repeat this offering, "Do this for a remembrance of me" (Luke 22:19). The Church's Eucharist is still celebrated to remember and respond to the gift of Jesus' own life.

On the way to the place of the agonized prayer, Jesus predicts that the Twelve will not be loyal to him but will scatter, as the prophet Zechariah had foretold (Mark 14:27, quoting Zechariah 13:7). Jesus reaches out in forgiveness to them and to all who will ever participate in this betrayal by promising to go before the Twelve into Galilee when God raises him from the dead (Mark 14:28).

Peter's cowardly denial forms a dramatic contrast to the loyalty of Jesus to the Father in his courageous confession of faith. The contrast is carefully narrated. While Peter is making himself comfortable by the fire, Jesus endures wearisome questioning. When Jesus loyally proclaims himself as God's son, Peter denies he even knew him. The self-confident leader of the Twelve is in need of salvation. Without the redeeming prayer of Jesus, not even the apostles can make an act of true and saving faith in Jesus and the Father.

The Theology Behind the Trials of Jesus

None of the disciples of Jesus attended his first trial, which was conducted by Jewish authorities. What the Synoptics provide is not a court record but a faith-filled interpretation of the motives inspiring Jesus to offer his life for the salvation of all human beings. The gospel accounts stress that Jesus was condemned by and for his own activity, not on the hearsay of others. In the face of dishonest witnesses, Jesus keeps silent. In desperation, the Jewish high priest calls upon him to explain his actions. As a result, Jesus is portrayed as constructing a powerful scriptural witness to his person and mission, which prompts the Jewish authority to declare, "He is deserving of death" (Matt 26:63-66).

In that exchange, Jesus proclaims first of all that he is the royal Messiah, the anointed heir of King David celebrated in Psalm 110 as greater than David himself. But beyond that, Jesus affirms that he is also the Son of Man, that mysterious apocalyptic figure portrayed in Daniel 7:13. Daniel had a vision of this figure receiving dominion and honor and glory from the Most High God. Jesus presents himself as receiving these honors and as reigning with the almighty God over the promised kingdom (Luke 22:66-71).

By this courageous self-presentation of his mission, Jesus provokes his rejection by his own. It is clear, then, that the dramatic revelation by Jesus of the so-called messianic secret, which was discussed in chapter 4, is the event that brings Jesus to his death in fulfillment of the Father's will. In response to that revelation, the assembled Jewish authorities decide to seek his death from the Roman governor, Pilate. His mission as Savior will not be complete until he is taken to the place of execution. The Father accepts this obedience of the Son of Man not as an execution but as a sacrifice, enabling sinners to find entrance to the kingdom of heaven.

The story of the trials is a striking illustration of the literary method of the gospel genre. It is a call to believers to identify with the loyal Jesus and to follow him to Calvary on a journey of faith. True faith blossoms into unbounded hope and joyful witness to God's saving power.

The Crucifixion of Jesus (Mark 15:21-47)

Mark's description of the death of Jesus (followed closely in its main points by Matthew) is extremely austere. It expresses the overwhelming desolation of the dying Jesus, cut off from all consolation, human and divine. Jesus is too weak to carry his own cross. The term "cross" here refers to the wooden horizontal beam to hold out the arms of the criminal. This beam was dragged to the place of execution by the condemned person.

On Calvary this crossbeam was dropped into the groove of the permanent horizontal beam of the cross, which remained fixed on the rocky hilltop. Jesus refuses to drink the wine mixed with myrrh to deaden his pain. Once raised up on the cross, Jesus is taunted by all classes of people going by, as well as by the criminals crucified at the same time.

On the cross Jesus endures three hours of physical and spiritual darkness. This suffering evokes from him the opening words of Psalm 22, a lament of a persecuted but upright worshiper of the Lord, "My God, my God, why have you forsaken me?" Jesus follows that lament with a wordless wail as he breathes his last breath.

Mark records an apocalyptic reaction, the splitting of the Temple veil "from top to bottom" (15:38), symbol of the profaning of its mysteries and the end of its sacred role. That sign proclaimed that the Jerusalem Temple is no longer the meeting place between the Lord and the chosen people.

At this point in his Gospel, Matthew inserts additional apocalyptic details to show the divine intervention. An earthquake occurs, rocks are split, tombs open, and the buried arise from

the dead. These dead persons appear in Jerusalem after the resurrection of Jesus (Matt 27:51-54).

The centurion standing guard at the crucifixion recognizes
God's intervention in what is happening to Jesus by saying,
"Surely, this man was God's son" (15:39). Mary Magdalen and
the other women who had followed Jesus from Galilee to take
care of his needs observe the happenings "from afar" (15:40).
Jesus is buried by Joseph of Arimathea (15:42-46). Again Matthew adds to the account. The Jews set a watch on the tomb of
Jesus, fearing that his predictions will come true. This apologetic
addition reflects hostility between Matthew's community and Jewish authorities (Matt 27:62-65).

Luke's Version of the Crucifixion (23:26-49)

The Gospel of Luke illustrates how the oral accounts of the
passion of Jesus had to be adapted to meet the special needs of
Gentile Christian converts. In describing the crucifixion, Luke
places emphasis on Jesus as model of human conduct. He walks
courageously to Calvary as exemplar of qualities that his disciples
need: confidence in God, compassion, forgiveness, and a spirit
of prayer. A man from Cyrene in North Africa, Simon, is pressed
into service to carry the wooden crossbeam "after Jesus." He thus
becomes the image of every disciple.

Jesus confidently tells the crowd of women following him not
to weep over him (23:26-31). And only Luke pictures Jesus as
praying for those who nailed him to the cross. As persecutions
increased in the Roman Empire, Christians had many occasions
to imitate their Lord's forgiving spirit. Again, only Luke includes
the incident of the repentant thief or revolutionary and his prayer
to be remembered in paradise. Jesus responds with an assurance
of God's powerful care, which will bring him into the kingdom
(23:39-43).

Jesus himself seems to determine the moment when his self-
sacrificing death will take place. He confidently speaks to his Father by using a verse from Psalm 31, "Into your hands I entrust
my spirit" (23:46). The centurion recognizes that Jesus was a "just
man," an innocent victim and faithful servant of his God. As
they depart, the witnesses speak for the whole world when they

acknowledge their guilt by striking their breasts. They recognize the loyalty of Jesus to his mission as a revelation of his perfect union with the heavenly Father (23:47-49).

Interpreting the Passion Today

A prayerful study of the passion narratives in the Synoptic Gospels of Matthew, Mark, and Luke enables us to enter into their role as religious interpretations of the saving power of the death of Jesus. They show that the saving work of Jesus is more than a past historical event. It is the turn of the ages, the transformation of humanity's relation to God. In dying Jesus reveals himself as loyal Son of God (Mark 15:39). His death shatters the veil of the Temple and makes available to all a new covenant in his blood.

The Gospels proclaim that the death of Jesus is an event of universal transforming consequences. These brief narratives communicate to us the depth of the profound religious experience of the early Christian communities. They have generated many theories of atonement over the course of the centuries. The Church does not define these theological interpretations but continues to proclaim and celebrate the mysteries of faith. The presence of God to this obedient Suffering Servant was the means that empowered Jesus to bring humanity to eternal life.

As literary creations inspired by the Holy Spirit, the Gospels offer believers authentic interpretations of the mystery of God reconciling humanity in his Son Jesus. He is the exemplary symbol and integrating core of all true discipleship. To be his disciple is to accept the cross; to accept the cross is to become his disciple.

The historical event of the death of Jesus on Calvary occurred only once, at a specific time and place in history. Yet it has universal implications, for it is the good news that frees both humanity as a whole and individual believers from the enslaving consequences of sin. The death of Jesus acts not simply as model to imitate but also as reconciling power that offers hope and peace to all in need.

Christians continue to speak the language of the cross by interiorizing the death of Jesus as their life principle in action.

Among the chief challenges in doing this are (1) to draw inspiration and encouragement from this death for personal and communal existence; (2) to make it the model of community consciousness and the source of direction in carrying out the responsibilities of how to live in the modern world; (3) to celebrate the death of Jesus in worship as the unifying force of healing for the world; and (4) to contemplate the gratuitous love inspiring it as the nourishment that feeds minds and hearts and frees human spirits.

The Father responded to the total love and obedience of Jesus by raising him from the dead. The risen Jesus is head of the Church and Lord of the new creation. The transforming existence the risen Jesus offers is able to incorporate believers into the one body of Christ. Our next chapter will show how the Gospels present the resurrection and exaltation of Jesus.

FOLLOW UP

The contemporary Scripture scholar who has devoted his talents to helping believers pray the narratives of Christ's passion is David M. Stanley, S.J. Readers will find guidance for interiorizing gospel narratives of the agony of Jesus in his book *Jesus in Gethsemane: The Early Church Reflects on the Sufferings of Jesus* (New York: Paulist, 1980). Robert J. Karris, *Luke: Artist and Theologian. Luke's Passion Account as Literature* (New York: Paulist, 1985) provides thematic reflections to show how Luke's artistry is a vehicle for his theological understanding of the death of Jesus.

10

The Resurrection Confirms
the Good News

In light of the importance that the resurrection of Jesus plays in the history of the Christian Church, the sobriety of the resurrection narratives in the Gospels is instructive. They were obviously not written to convince readers about the reality of the event. On the contrary, the way the three Synoptic Gospels describe key elements of this mystery of the victory of Jesus over sin and death assumes deep faith in those being addressed. The risen Jesus was already the basis of the new mode of life their readers enjoyed.

Matthew, Mark, and Luke all express the climax of the good news in the form of resurrection narratives. They form the fifth and final element of the shaping principle of the gospel genre, which was explained in chapter 3. The Father placed his seal of approval on the entire ministry of Jesus by raising him from the dead. This chapter will show how each Synoptic Gospel narrates this response of God to the fidelity of Jesus in keeping with its own theology and target audience.

No one witnessed the resurrection of Jesus. It was not an event within the sphere of reality subject to human observation but occurred in the realm of spiritual reality that may be called "salvation history," the divine plan or the mystery of salvation. In other words, the resurrection is not an event subject to the limitations of time and space and able to be measured by physical instruments. A mystery must be revealed by God, and it can be accepted as real only by the grace of faith.

How did the gospel writers arrive at a means of narrating the resurrection? They depended upon an oral tradition that first described the new relation Jesus established with his original disciples and the changes this relation brought about in them. The resurrection accounts enable us to see that these changes were the result of divine activity rather than the products of purely human initiative. Because the relationship of believers to the risen Jesus was an entirely new human experience, no language already existing was adequate to communicate the new reality.

The first witnesses of the risen Jesus had to stretch human language to make expressions that were capable of naming this divine activity that took place in Jesus. These early witnesses began to coin terms that conveyed the double tension the resurrection produced in them, namely, a sense of continuity between the risen and the earthly Jesus and the experience of discontinuity between the risen Jesus and his past earthly condition of weakness.

Continuity. In terms of continuity, the resurrection meant that the glorious Lord who reigns with the Father is the same Jesus whose missionary activity these witnesses shared. When finally translated into narrative form, this continuity of existence between the two modes of existence took the form of the resurrection appearances. Once the risen Jesus empowered humans to experience him as still very much present and active, the disciples recognized him as the same Jesus who called and taught them and who offered his life for them and for all.

Discontinuity. The discontinuity of the risen Jesus with his earthly status was eventually translated into the scenes of the empty tomb. The disappearance of the body of Jesus from the tomb without a trace points to the liberation of Jesus from this creation and the total transformation of his being in the new age. The glorified Lord remains available to the faithful as truly human, able to relate to the needs of all who need salvation. Yet this Jesus is also reigning in glory at the right hand of the Father as Lord of the universe.

When believers proclaim that Jesus is Lord, they designate him as fulfilling for them the same role that Yahweh, the Lord of Israel, performed for his chosen people in the Mosaic covenant. Hence, in the risen Jesus the word "lives" takes on a new, transcendent meaning. As glorified Lord, he is life giving, communicating his transforming power to believers. A look at the three resurrection narratives in Mark, Matthew, and Luke will illustrate how the gospel accounts communicate the mystery of the victory of Jesus over death.

But before dealing with the gospel accounts, it is necessary to look at the long literary process that lies behind them.

Growth of the Resurrection Stories

Without the resurrection, no gospel could exist. Unless the Father had showed his approval of the mission of Jesus by raising him up, no Christian community would have come into existence and no evangelization would have begun. A rapid reading of the gospel accounts of the resurrection events may give the impression that they are a chronicle of events describing a brief stay of Jesus on earth before returning to the Father, in the event that Luke dramatizes as the ascension. But a careful analysis of the resurrection narratives reveals that they are of an entirely different nature.

The resurrection narratives are the final result of a long period of reflection, beginning with the first witnesses. They grew out of an articulation of the awareness that came over the apostles as they wrestled with the mystery of the glorification of Jesus. The first step was their ability to express that awareness in terms meaningful to their fellow disciples of the earthly Jesus. From that point the journey of the composition of the narratives now found in the three Synoptic Gospels involved three stages:

Stage 1. The apostles, under the guidance of the Holy Spirit and drawing upon their personal experience of a new, transcendent presence of Jesus, developed a vocabulary that expressed this mystery in human terminology. This seemingly impossible task was the triumph of faith empowered by divine revelation and the gift of the Spirit of the risen Lord. The accounts indicate that even the apostles, who enjoyed the company of the earthly Jesus, could not easily grasp the transformation that had taken place within his whole being. They had to fill out simple expressions of faith with a new depth of meaning.

The key phrases of this first stage were three: (1) Jesus lives; (2) Jesus is raised up; (3) Jesus is exalted.

1. The phrase "Jesus lives" does not mean that the risen Jesus returned to the same earthly condition he had before he died, as if by resuscitation. Rather, it means that Jesus is truly alive but not with the kind of life humans on earth experience, subject to historical uncertainty and death. He now lives in the eschatological new age, in a condition beyond the power of death to affect or limit in any way.

2. This new form of existence is also expressed in the second statement, phrased to describe his condition of glory: "Jesus is raised up," that is, he is taken out of the state in which he was subject to death. Jesus now enjoys a form of reality that death cannot harm. He transcends historical limits and has power over time and space.

3. The third phrase, "Jesus is exalted," captures another aspect of the new mode of presence Jesus enjoys. The power of the heavenly Father has elevated Jesus into the role of lordship over all creation, with the promise of divine friendship for those who believe in his saving mission.

For the eyewitnesses of the risen Jesus, these three phrases were effective in deepening the experience of Jesus as exercising a transforming influence in their lives. Equally important, they provided the means by which eyewitnesses were able to communicate their privileged experience to other persons who wanted to join their quest for the kingdom of God.

Stage 2. As the eyewitnesses grew in faith, they traveled around to bear witness and to share their unique experience of the risen Lord with others and to invite them into the growing community. They preached "conversion unto the remission of sins" in the name of Jesus (Luke 24:47). The Holy Spirit touched the hearts of both Jews and Gentiles to accept the gift of faith and to confess, "Jesus is Lord." The believing community soon spread throughout the Roman Empire.

These Christian believers came together for prayer and the celebration of the Lord's Supper. In the face of opposition they supported one another in the love of Christ. Profound spiritual growth gave witness that Jesus remains active in the world through the working of his Spirit. Part of the liturgy of these communities of prayer was to celebrate the risen Jesus in glory and yet still present to them. The two types of narratives that translated the faith embodied in those key phrases of the first stage were stories about the finding of the empty tomb and accounts of the appearances of the risen Jesus.

Stage 3. When the evangelists were composing their Gospels, they incorporated both types of narratives about the risen Jesus into these new literary creations. This mode of development illustrates my insistence that these accounts were not chronicles to describe a period of time Jesus spent visiting with his disciples. Rather, they are narratives of revelation.

The Gospels of the resurrection, then, convey the meaning of the victory of Jesus over death. It is a victory not for Jesus alone but for all believers. This purpose guards us against trying to reconstruct historical scenarios of the resurrection experiences. The entire narratives are religious: theological, hortatory, and saving. They cannot be understood except in confession and obedience.

Faith in the risen Jesus roots the life of the Church in realities beyond this world. Faith demanded of the apostolic eyewitnesses and still demands of modern believers, individually and collectively, certain basic choices in life-style, symbolized in taking up the cross. For Christians, cross and resurrection can never be separated.

The resurrection of Jesus proclaimed that his choice of the cross was not only pleasing to his Father but also brings justification, or friendship, with the Father to all who put their trust in him as Savior. The power of his resurrection maintains the vital tension between the sense of alienation from the world's selfish spirit and the generous outreach toward human need. Like the Master, believers portray a spirit that is both free and compassionate toward a hostile world.

Empty Tomb Narrative in Mark (16:1-8)

In keeping with the austerity of his portrait of Jesus, Mark ends with a brief narrative of the finding of the empty tomb of Jesus by three of his female disciples. In the tomb is a young man dressed in a luminous flowing robe. He reminds the women of the promise of Jesus to go before his disciples into Galilee (see 14:28). He tells them to let the disciples, and Peter in particular, know about the resurrection of Jesus.

Mark ends his Gospel there abruptly. Instead of reporting the incident, the women run away, "for they were afraid." This surprise ending sets the tone for the Church as a pilgrim community destined never to be at home on this earth. Yet it remains hope filled, confident that its destiny lies in reunion with the risen Lord, who has gone ahead to the Father.

The remainder of the Gospel of Mark (16:9-20) is usually set apart from the rest in modern editions. This printing device signifies that this conclusion was not part of the original plan of the evangelist but was an early addition of the faith community. Readers can recognize that it is a summary, formed by combining elements of the appearance accounts found in the Gospels of Matthew, Luke, and John. This addition (so early that it is part of the official or canonical Church edition) indicates how important the resurrection appearances are for the believing community.

The gospel story is incomplete without belief in the heavenly exaltation and yet abiding presence of Jesus to believers. That paradoxical belief does not come easily. It is a gift of God, who alone can lead his creatures into the realm of faith, into that new age over which Jesus rules as Lord.

The resurrection of Jesus is a powerful combination of past, present, and future into a dynamic unity. The same Jesus who called and formed the first apostles is present to the Church as saving Lord, forming and sustaining witnesses until the end of time. His presence permeates all dimensions of the believer's existence: body and spirit, intelligence and emotions, will and imagination. Faith recognizes the glorified Jesus as Lord of the new age, destined to receive honor and glory and praise from all creation.

The Church celebrates its response of faith in the Lord Jesus in a variety of ways: in liturgy, in preaching the good news of salvation, in its mission of compassion and healing. The community's task in the world is to make available the power and wisdom of the glorified Lord, to complete the mission of the incarnation. Members of the Church are destined to bear the marks of his suffering and rejection because they follow his example in offering hope to the world.

Such hope does not spring from any human accomplishment. The apostles did not pick themselves up by their bootstraps after the crucifixion. Only after Jesus rose and sent his life-giving Spirit upon this weak and fearful group did they become witnesses of the gospel. The Spirit created a totally new interior dynamism so that these disciples could experience and share their faith that Jesus was now with the Father and yet still with them.

Matthew Transforms the Empty Tomb Account (28:1-15)

Matthew's Gospel is addressed primarily to converts from Judaism. It incorporates an apologetic approach in the form of many polemic elements. Evidently, his community faced opposition from Jewish synagogues competing for the allegiance of law-abiding Jews. This conflict accounts for certain additions to the story of the finding of the empty tomb.

Matthew describes the breaking open of tombs after the death of Jesus (27:52-53). He also notes that after the resurrection an earthquake took place and an angel appeared (28:2). He tells how the Jewish leaders tried to cover up the victory of Jesus over death by bribing the guards to say that his followers stole his body (28:11-15).

In spite of these characteristic apocalyptic and polemic additions, Matthew still presents the resurrection event as a mystery. No one saw it take place. It is beyond human power to describe, and its impact permeates all levels of reality. The earthquake signifies its cosmic dimensions. In Jesus, a new heaven and a new earth come into existence. The angel in gleaming robes illustrates the awesome power of this mystery to transform the lives of believers. It transports them into the divine realm and empowers them to share the victory of Jesus.

Matthew's constant concern in composing his Gospel is to strengthen Jewish Christians who are under attack for their new faith. Their fellow Jews accused Jesus of being unfaithful to their ancestral heritage. They sought to discredit Christians by circulating rumors denying the reality of the resurrection. To counter this propaganda, Matthew puts in his apologetic explanation of the hostility of Jesus' own people to him. These details illustrate how the primitive narrative could be enriched to encourage Christians to be faithful to the mystery of the resurrection.

The victory of God over death in and through Jesus is crucial for humans to attain their destiny. At the same time, salvation is not a work of magic. The resurrection teaches believers that they must be converted and live in newness of life. Matthew presents that challenge in the final dramatic scene of his Gospel.

The Great Commission of Matthew (28:16-20)

In many ways the whole Gospel of Matthew is a preparation for its final scene, the great commission. The way it describes the activity of Jesus in his public life as gradually empowering the disciples prepares readers for his act of handing over all his power and teaching authority to them after the resurrection.

The infancy narrative reveals that Jesus should bear the name Immanuel, meaning "God with us." After the resurrection Jesus comes back to his disciples to teach why he was given that name. He will no longer be present to the world in visible bodily form. Yet he still remains with believers in the saving ministry of the Church to all humanity.

This final scene pictures the eleven apostles as believing in the risen Jesus even before they see him. They immediately recognize him as he manifests himself in Galilee, and they fall down in homage. Yet even at this moment, "some of them doubted" (28:17). This mysterious comment is perhaps better translated in English as "yet they hesitated." The act of faith in the risen Lord is always a free act and a dangerous decision. God attracts but does not force the human will to believe. Awesome as the resurrection is, it remains an invitation.

To this small group of eager and yet still fearful disciples, Jesus addresses the great commission in three parts:

1. As a revelation. "All authority in heaven and on earth has been given to me." Jesus spent his whole life exercising his authority as Son of Man to teach and to heal, even to forgive sin. He revealed that authority to his disciples only gradually and shared part of it with them. Now he displays its full scope. It extends throughout "heaven and earth," which is the Hebrew way of say-

ing to every part of the universe. Jesus is now joined to his Father as universal Savior and ruler over the world. He relates to all creatures in a transcendent way without limitation of time or space. That is his unique power as risen Lord. Now Jesus begins to exercise that power in a new way.

2. As a commission. Jesus reveals that he is going to identify his Church fully with his saving mission. During his earthly mission Jesus limited his teaching and healing to the house of Israel. Now his disciples are commissioned to extend his teaching and discipleship to the whole human race by offering the gift of faith to all. Those who accept this revelation will celebrate their allegiance publicly by receiving the sacrament of baptism. Baptism symbolizes the incorporation of believers into the community of Father, Son, and Holy Spirit.

Since the Gospel of Matthew has said nothing about the outpouring of the Holy Spirit upon the disciples, this scene is best understood as a telescoping of the process by which the Church came to articulate its belief in the mystery of the divine oneness of the Father, Jesus, and the Spirit. Only the experience of the indwelling of the Holy Spirit within the first eyewitnesses of the resurrection and then within other believers and the community as a whole makes such a profession of faith possible.

3. As a promise. The Gospel ends by explaining why the angel told Joseph that the child to be born would be called Immanuel, "God with us." He continues to make God present in the world in and through his Church. Loyalty to the Church is loyalty to Jesus. Those who enter the community enjoy the blessings of this glorious presence. Through his Spirit, Jesus is even more real and powerfully present to believers than he was to his disciples on earth. He continues to fulfill the Law and the Prophets and to prevail over the forces of Satan.

The Appearance Narratives in Luke (24:13-53)

Luke's Gentile converts were interested in knowing how the risen Jesus impacted upon their lives. How does the mystery of the resurrection affirm the abiding, saving, and transforming presence of the Lord Jesus in their daily existence? Jesus has passed from being within the confines of human history to a new mode of existence. Does Jesus in glory remain aloof or isolated from the human condition? How can he come into continuous intimate contact with believers and associate them in his saving mission?

The appearance narratives in Luke address these questions. Jesus had to take the initiative in revealing his new mode of existence and making his presence felt. Luke distinguishes two types of appearances, an official visit of Jesus to the disciples assembled as a group, and a private appearance to two disciples on their way to Emmaus.

The first type illustrates the role of the mystery of the resurrection in respect to the Church as a whole and its mission in the world. Like the meeting of Jesus and his disciples on the mountain in Galilee related by Matthew, the visit of the risen Jesus to his disciples in Jerusalem described by Luke culminates in a commission. They are to carry on his work of preaching and reconciliation among all peoples. The second type of appearance offers a model for sacramental encounters with the risen Lord.

Luke links both forms of appearances, public and private, to a meal with Jesus and his explanation of how Scripture is fulfilled in him. Luke thus locates the mystery of the resurrection in the context of the history of salvation. The meal reminds the Church that the risen Jesus is present in a communication of power and wisdom in the Eucharistic breaking of bread. From their community, sacrament-sharing believers receive the strength to bear witness to Jesus in this world.

When Jesus spoke to the two disciples at Emmaus, he explained that what happened to him was the fulfillment of the message of every part of Scripture. This scene in one sense telescopes the early Church's missionary apologetic for preaching to both Jews and Gentiles. The cross is a scandal for those who cannot see it in context of the overarching divine plan of salvation.

Under the guidance of the Holy Spirit, whom the risen Jesus sent upon them, the infant communities worked out a program and an apologia for their new way of life. Christians began to read the entire Hebrew Bible in the light of the life, teaching, death, and resurrection of Jesus. They found him everywhere in the Scriptures: in the Law, in the Prophets, in the Wisdom Writings, called "Psalms" in Luke 24:44.

The two disciples run back from Emmaus to Jerusalem to tell the other disciples about their meeting with the risen Lord. As they are speaking, Jesus appears to the apostolic band. The in-breaking of Jesus creates an overwhelming impact. Luke describes the disciples as "frightened and terrified" (24:37). Jesus has to reassure them and prepare them to become "witnesses of these events," promising to empower them by sending the Holy Spirit upon them (24:48-49).

The risen Jesus communicates to this fearful group the gift of peace, and not in the superficial sense of a banal "hello." His peace is grace, power to preach and to offer "repentance and remission of sins to all nations" (24:47). They are then able to go forth and to witness "with great joy" and to devote themselves to praising God (24:52-53).

Experiencing the Resurrection Today

The Gospels show that the early Christians came to know the mystery of the resurrection of Jesus not by some kind of scientific verification. Rather, the glorified Jesus poured his own Holy Spirit into their hearts to transform their consciousness and their lives. This Spirit, living in them, made the Church the witness to a new reality, the new age.

This gift of the Holy Spirit is decisive in the Church's ongoing experience of the mystery of the resurrection. The Spirit must bridge the profound gap that exists between those few disciples who were eyewitnesses of the risen Jesus and the millions of believers who came later, including all contemporary believers. If they are to experience the risen Lord in their lives, the source must be the sanctifying presence of his Spirit.

As I said at the beginning of this chapter, the resurrection narratives act as the final element in the shaping principle of the gospel form. They communicate the Father's approval of the mission of Jesus. That approval is effective, performative. It is the divine power making the mission of Jesus become a saving reality for all who commit their lives to him. And that is what the gift of the Spirit of the risen Jesus is for the Church. The Spirit is light for those groping against the darkness of despair and alienation. The Spirit is strength for those needing courage to resist the stranglehold of sin.

Acts of the Apostles shows the working of the Holy Spirit in those early Christians who took the good news to all parts of the Roman Empire and beyond. Only because they experienced this freeing, life-giving presence were these early believers able to give witness to the mystery of the resurrection. They attracted fellow witnesses, established new communities, and often laid down their lives for the sake of the gospel. The power of the resurrection is celebrated throughout the New Testament, from the letters of Paul to the writings of the gospels.

In reading the gospel accounts of the resurrection, it is helpful to keep in mind that they were written after the letters of Paul to the communities he founded and served. As I show in the earlier chapters of this book, the gospels build upon the special vocabulary and religious experience of primitive Christian communities. They are theologically inspired narratives rather than "biographies" of the Lord Jesus on earth and risen to glory.

The exalted Lord Jesus is more than an inspiration to the Church and to individual believers. He is the heart and soul of all faith, love, and hope. Even more: through his Spirit the exalted Jesus makes the believing community the saving leaven to transform the world. He was foreshadowed in the covenant of Sinai. He nourishes believers through his Spirit, present in the sacraments. He is the light of the world through the preaching and service of his Church till the end of time.

Finally, the risen Jesus is a visible pledge that our bodies too are destined to be transformed, in such a way that they will have a share in God's friendship and in the celebration of the heavenly banquet forever.

FOLLOW UP

The mystery of the resurrection is central to the gospel. It is a mystery that believers turn to again and again for nourishment and hope. An inspiring and comprehensive treatment of this mystery in its biblical roots and ethical dimensions is the study of Xavier Léon-Dufour, *Resurrection and the Message of Easter* (New York: Holt, Rinehart and Winston, 1974). A more technical theological approach is found in Gerald O'Collins, *Jesus Risen: An Historical, Fundamental and Systematic Examination of Christ's Resurrection* (New York: Paulist, 1987).

11

John: The Spiritual Gospel

The shaping principle of the literary form gospel, described in chapter 3, underwent a parallel development in the Fourth Gospel, attributed to John. This development illustrates how a reflective or contemplative community was able to produce a Gospel that has distinctive features and yet portrays the Jesus familiar to believers from the Synoptics.

Like Luke, the Gospel of John has a prologue, but a more elaborate one. It is a theological summary of the Gospel. The prologue answers the questions, Who is Jesus? Why is Jesus important? Its answer begins not by tracing the earthly origins of Jesus but by a poetic description of the realm where the Eternal dwells. There with the Father is his infinite Word, already enjoying personal community.

The Fourth Gospel uses the geometric figure of the parabola to portray the story of this unique relationship between the Father and the Word in eternity and in time. The story begins in the infinite beyond, in the divine glory that lies beyond all finite coordinates of the parabola. Out of this glorious world, the Word "was coming" into the human family as God's creative and saving presence until he actually took human existence as Jesus (1:14). During his brief stay on earth, this transcendent Jesus conducts himself as a mirror in which God's covenant qualities of loyalty and mercy are reflected. These were already anticipated in God's appearance to Moses on Mount Sinai (1:14, 17). The brief earthly ministry of Jesus forms the main part of the parabola described in the Gospel of John as a revelation of the Father's love and glory. After Jesus finishes this earthly mission, he returns to the infinite realm of God, now as the glorified Redeemer who empowers all who receive him in faith to become children of God (1:12).

This poetic prologue is balanced by a longer narrative, which completes the introduction to the Fourth Gospel (1:19-51). John gradually reveals Jesus through a series of testimonies by people who greet Jesus in a variety of titles. These meetings are described as occupying a period of a week, symbolizing the first week of the new creation.

The first person Jesus encounters is John the Baptizer, who recognizes him with the mysterious title "Lamb of God who takes away the sin of the world" (1:29). Out of reverence for Jesus, the Fourth Gospel does not record either the baptizing of Jesus by John or his testing in the desert as God's Son. This omission stretches the shaping principle of Gospel to its limit and marks the final stage of the apostolic Church's efforts to embody the mystery of redemptive incarnation in narrative form.

This narrative introduction ends with the first revelation of the glory of Jesus at the wedding at Cana. There, the first witnesses that Jesus attracted in Judea see his glory, which will be revealed progressively in this Gospel by a series of signs evoking belief. The Fourth Gospel, then, functions like a cosmic legal trial in which God and Satan, light and darkness, contest for the loyalty of human beings. Readers must choose for or against Jesus. Those who believe in him are judged worthy of eternal life.

The remainder of John's Gospel consists of the remaining three elements of the shaping principle found in the Synoptics: revelation in word and deed, rejection by humans, approval of Jesus by God. The Fourth Gospel presents these elements in the form of a series of signs that God is working in and through Jesus. One of the great commentators on the Fourth Gospel, C. H. Dodd, divides the remainder into two parts: the Book of Signs (John 2-12) and the Book of Glory (John 13-21). By "sign" Dodd means the characteristic literary unit in the Fourth Gospel. A sign consists of two parts: a revelatory deed of Jesus, not necessarily miraculous, followed by some form of discourse in which Jesus explains this dimension of his saving work. The Fourth Gospel thus represents a parallel tradition to the Synoptics by an unknown author identified in tradition as John, a dramatic genius. In line with tradition, I use the terms Gospel of John and Fourth Gospel interchangeably.

The Book of Signs

Rather than multiplying scenes from the ministry of Jesus as do the Synoptic evangelists, John prefers to select a small number of events capable of revealing Jesus as sign of God's saving purpose. John portrays Jesus as acting in perfect intimacy with his Father to convince his own people that "God so loved the world that he gave his only Son so that all who entrust their life to the Son will not perish but will have eternal life. For God did not send his Son into the world to judge the human race but that the human race would be liberated through him" (3:16-17).

The final stage in the coming of the Word of God, summarized in the prologue, is later described in the image of an apprenticed Son, introduced in 5:19-20 and elaborated in Trinitarian language in 5:21-30. Like a master craftsman, God undertakes to communicate all his trade secrets to his Son so that the Son too may become the master artist, sharing his Father's skill in giving eternal life to mortals. This self-giving of the Father is complete when he raises Jesus from the dead and enthrones him in heavenly glory. Then the Father and Son join in sending the Holy Spirit upon believers to complete the parabolic journey of the Word from the lap of the Father back to eternal glory, now joined by all believers.

The Book of Signs links the mighty deeds of Jesus to the great Jewish feasts, which celebrate God's saving work for the chosen people. Jesus begins within a Jewish setting to extend salvation to the whole world. This literary setting clarifies the nature of these signs. They are not magic deeds performed to dazzle spectators. Rather, they are symbolic actions that portray God coming to save his people. The following brief explanations show that each sign is, in some fashion, the whole revelation. Each one emphasizes some element of the good news of God's saving presence in Jesus and calls readers to trust and conversion. Each one is a carefully polished gem that reveals some facet of the incarnation. Taken together, these signs call the community to celebrate the mystery that "Jesus is the Christ, the Son of God" (20:31). Each member can thereby contemplate these scenes and by believing have life in his name.

The Sign of Cana (2:1-11)

The Fourth Gospel reduces the Galilean ministry of Jesus, which occupies the first half of Mark's Gospel, to three short scenes: the Cana sign with a visit to Capernaum (2:1-12); the cure of the son of a royal official (4:46-54); and the multiplication of the loaves and fishes with a sea rescue and subsequent preaching (6:1-7:9).

After gathering five witnesses during a visit to John the Baptizer along the Jordan river in Judea, Jesus brings them to Galilee to a village where a wedding is in progress. The confusion of the opening remarks as well as the grammar of the opening sentence in Greek illustrates that John works from sources. He splices them together without removing all the seams, for example, a plural subject with a singular verb (2:2). And then, how could the disciples of Jesus have been invited to this wedding when no one in Galilee knew about their existence? Such a lack of smooth transitions is common in the Fourth Gospel, which skips from place to place without warning. Such freedom points to an audience of believers anxious to witness to Jesus as the only Son of God.

A marriage feast is an appropriate opening scene for the Gospel that is filled with symbols of fulfillment. This scene introduces three key themes that will reappear often: revelatory sign, glory, and the act of believing. When the group with Jesus arrives, his mother, who is never designated by her personal name in the Fourth Gospel, assumes the central role. She is shocked at seeing this group of hungry men barging into the village celebration. Their appetites threaten the fragile hospitality. These two families had planned the wedding for months, carefully hoarding their limited supplies to avoid the shame of falling short in public.

Mary quickly assumes her role as mother to gently urge Jesus to move on with the reminder, "They have no wine" (2:3). The dwindling supply cannot match the thirst of six men who have been on the road for three days. This opening scene is very down to earth. Jesus does not let events stay on this plain. His answer comes in the form of a double question, a technique found elsewhere in the Fourth Gospel. The purpose is to inform his mother that Jesus has entered a new stage in his mission.

The first question uses an idiom found a few times in the Hebrew Scriptures and in two scenes found in the Synoptics, "What to me and to thee?" In more idiomatic English, this means, "What is our relationship?" (see Mark 1:24 and Luke 4:34; Matt 8:29; Mark 5:7; Luke 8:28). It is one of those sayings that adapts to different contexts. In both Synoptic scenes it is addressed by demons about to be expelled by Jesus. They resent his divine power to drive them out of human bodies. By contrast, at Cana Jesus uses it to alert his mother to recognize that he is beginning a new stage in his mission. He invites Mary to change her way of relating to him and points to her new role by using the term "woman." Readers can understand why by recalling that John's prologue opened with the first words of Hebrew Scripture, "In the beginning." In this context, Jesus invites Mary to perform the role of the woman of Genesis 1:18-23, the woman destined to become the helper of Adam in ruling creation.

Mary is a faithful disciple and grasps this role when Jesus poses the second question, "Hasn't my hour come?" Unfortunately many texts translate this as a statement in spite of the way the action is moving. Jesus is alerting Mary that this is the moment for him to begin the revelation that will end in his glorification through the cross and return to the Father. Mary immediately enlists the support of the waiters by telling them, "Do whatever he tells you" (2:5). In her command Mary employs another biblical response, taken from the Joseph story in Genesis. Joseph had predicted the seven fruitful and seven barren years and convinced the Pharaoh to stock up grain. When famine arrived and the people appealed for their grain, the Pharaoh said, "Go to Joseph. Do whatever he tells you." Mary thus enters into the saving plan of God as the first believer of the new creation.

Jesus then performs his first sign, a symbolic act that "revealed his glory, and his disciples believed in him" (2:11). This conclusion makes clear why John portrays the disciples as being invited to the wedding. They are destined to be witnesses to all the signs of Jesus. Their preaching will lead those who did not encounter the earthly Jesus to the heavenly marriage feast of glory.

The Sign of the Temple (2:13-22)

Only in John's Gospel does Jesus go to Jerusalem, the holy city of the Jews, at the beginning of his public ministry. There, angered by trafficking in the Temple, Jesus drives out the merchants who are defiling "my Father's house" (2:16). When challenged on this, Jesus in turn challenges his opponents to destroy this "sanctuary," and he will rebuild it in three days (2:19). John comments that Jesus was using "sanctuary" as an image of his own body, which would be raised up in the resurrection (2:21-22). This brief dramatic encounter is also a sign of the glory of Jesus to deepen belief in his followers.

It is followed by two encounters that describe Jesus revealing his glory. The first revelation is to a Jewish leader, Nicodemus the Pharisee, who remains hesitant at this time. Later Nicodemus will stand forth as defender of the rights of Jesus (7:51) and finally as the loyal disciple who buries the body of Jesus in a new tomb (19:39-41). The second encounter is with a Samaritan woman, heretical to the Jews, whom Jesus meets on his way back to Galilee. He engages her in conversation about God's will and reveals to her that he is the expected Messiah (4:25-26). He stays with this heretical group, and they witness that he is "truly the Savior of the world" (4:42).

Cure of the Son of the Official (4:46-53)

This sign of the power of Jesus takes place on his return to Galilee. It is similar to a healing found in Matthew 8:5-13 and Luke 7:1-10. But in the Fourth Gospel, Jesus objects to the emphasis on physical cures and asks petitioners to believe that he can give life. When the Gentile official believes that Jesus has cured his son from afar, "He himself believed and his whole household" (4:53). This response is similar to the action of the jailer in Philippi (Acts 16:31-34). The event is described like a conversion experience leading to baptism in early Church preaching.

Cure of the Cripple at the Pool (5:1-9)

Jesus immediately returns to Jerusalem for an unnamed Jewish feast. He encounters a man who has waited among the infirm at the pool of Bethesda for thirty-eight years without being cured.

The word of Jesus brings immediate physical healing, but the spiritual significance of the event becomes clear only in the accompanying words of Jesus. At this point Jesus refuses to bear witness to himself (5:31) but appeals to the testimony of John the Baptizer (5:32) and to the works that his Father sent him to accomplish, to his mission and to the Scripture that comes from the lawgiver Moses (5:46-47).

Bread in the Desert and Walking on the Lake (6:1-21)

Quickly the scene shifts back to Galilee, where Jesus feeds a crowd of five thousand from five barley loaves and two small fishes. John notes that this sign took place near the Passover, the feast celebrating liberation from slavery in Egypt. Jesus fed this large crowd by invoking a divine blessing upon the first fruits of the year's barley harvest. As usual, Jesus does not let the sign point only to physical nourishment. His discourse reveals that he is the Bread of Life, nourishment for all who believe in him. This promise foreshadows his ability to be present to people separated from him in time and space through a sharing in the Eucharist. Jesus reinforces this message by making himself present to his disciples as they struggle with a sudden storm on the Lake of Galilee.

Interlude of Confrontation (7:1-8:59)

Before narrating the next sign, John conveys a sense of the ongoing conflicts between Jesus and the leadership of the chosen people by describing a series of confrontations. These take place in the context of the autumn feast of Tents in Jerusalem and use images from its liturgy: a water offering on the last day of the feast and the great torches that light up the Temple area. Jesus alludes to the water offering when he cries out, "If anyone of you is thirsty, come to me. Let the one who believes drink of me. As Scripture says, 'Flowing waters will pour out of one's insides' " (7:38). John adds a footnote identifying this water as the Holy Spirit, available to believers only after the death and resurrection of Jesus.

Jesus also draws upon the ceremony of lighting the Temple with torches by proclaiming, "I am the light of the world" (8:12). Jesus now bears witness to himself. He defends his change of tactics as based on the knowledge he has of his origin and destiny, namely, to come from and go into the Father's presence.

This long series of controversies ends with a special form of interchange that John often employs, "revelation patterns" (8:31-59). These are not simple dialogues but rather an interchange made up of three elements. First, Jesus reveals a religious truth, often in cryptic fashion. Second, the interlocutor misunderstands or challenges his statement. Third, Jesus clarifies his opening revelation. The common theme that runs through this series of six revelation patterns is the difference between Jesus and Abraham, who is mentioned in John only here. His name appears ten times—hardly an accident.

Jesus' bold affirmation at the end of this series of revelations is that Abraham rejoiced to see his coming. The opponents violently deny such a thing is possible. Jesus responds with the final dramatic revelation, "Amen, amen I tell you: before Abraham came to be, I AM" (8:58). This allusion to the way the Lord revealed himself to Moses almost costs Jesus his life, and he is forced to flee.

The Sign of the Light of the World (9:1-41)

Unexpectedly, Jesus next appears walking with his disciples in Jerusalem, where he sees a blind man. This sickness raises a theological question among his disciples: Is this blindness the result of the man's personal sin or the effect of inherited guilt? Jesus rejects these popular theories and says it is for the glory of God. He tells the blind man, a beggar, to wash in the pool of Siloam, the only source of water in the city. This action initiates the discourse part of the sign, a series of seven dramatic scenes in which the Jewish leaders force the man to choose for or against Jesus. When he accepts Jesus as a prophet sent by God, the beggar is "expelled from the synagogue" (9:22). By this technical term John makes him a symbol of Christians who are being forced out of Jewish cult at the time the Fourth Gospel is being composed because they were acknowledging Jesus as "the Son of Man" (9:35).

Without a change in setting, Jesus suddenly starts speaking in new imagery. He proclaims his identity in two metaphors linked to Jewish tradition, namely, "gate" to the kingdom of God and "shepherd" of God's people, leading them to freedom. Jesus carries out these roles not in opposition to God but as the Son loved by the Father for laying down his life for human beings (10:17). The crowd again tries to stone Jesus because they refuse to believe that Jesus is in the Father and the Father in him (10:38). A second time he flees from them, now across the Jordan River.

Sign of the Risen Life (11:1–12:19)

As the final sign performed during the public preaching of Jesus, John uses a series of six dramatic scenes to describe an event not recorded in any Synoptic Gospel. This is the raising to life of Lazarus, brother of Mary and Martha. They send for Jesus when Lazarus becomes ill, but he delays going until after the brother has died, "so that I may wake him up" (11:11). After the recent attempts on the life of Jesus, his disciples are fearful about going to their village of Bethany near Jerusalem. As in all the signs, John is interested in the physical rising only insofar as it reveals the glory of Jesus and evokes belief. The words of Jesus to Martha, "If you believe, you will see the glory of God" (11:40), recall the close of the first sign of Cana, "He manifested his glory and his disciples believed in him" (2:11).

Thus, the Book of Signs returns to the note that opened it. The gospel demands decision; the reader must make a choice for or against Jesus. John reports that the chief priests and Pharisees call a meeting of the leadership "because this man is performing many signs" (11:47). They decide that he must be sacrificed "for the sake of the people, lest the whole nation perish" (11:50). John notes that this remark is a prophecy of the real meaning of the death of Jesus, which is reconciliation of all humanity to God.

Final Appearance in Jerusalem

The phrase "six days before the Passover" (12:1), the day the Passover lamb is chosen, sets the tone for the remainder of "the spiritual Gospel." By going into Jerusalem on that day, Jesus placed himself in the position of being chosen as victim for the unique Passover celebration on Calvary. The presence of Jesus attracts a large crowd of Jewish pilgrims to welcome him as "king of the Jews," a role Jesus avoided after feeding the crowd in the desert (6:15). Now Jesus accepts this title, but on his own terms.

Jesus gives this role new meaning by a symbolic action. "Finding an ass and sitting upon it," Jesus fulfills the prophetic vision that Zion's king would come not in military might but as a meek leader (12:14-15).

This is the first of a series of fulfillment texts John uses to explain that the passion of Jesus happened in accord with God's saving plan and with the foreknowledge of Jesus. John also emphasizes the universal impact of the death of Jesus by introducing a delegation of Greek-speaking Jews who want to see Jesus. His response is to announce his coming death under the image of the dying of a seed that "will bear much fruit" (12:24).

Then Jesus pours out an intimate prayer to the Father. "Now is my soul shaken and what shall I say? Will it be, 'Father, save me from this hour?' But I came precisely for this hour. I will say, 'Father, glorify your name' " (12:27-28). This is John's version of the prayer recorded in the Synoptics in the agony scene. John places it in a public setting and gives the Father's response. God accepts the self-offering of Jesus: "I did glorify it [no doubt, in sending the Word to become human in Jesus] and I will again glorify it [in accepting your offering on the cross]" (12:28).

Why does John picture the Father consoling Jesus in this fashion? Because from now on Jesus will be in complete charge of events, almost as having returned to the Father in the infinity of the parabola from which the Word came. Jesus predicts his death on the cross for the third time (12:32; see 3:14; 8:28—comparable to the passion predictions of the Synoptics in different circumstances). Jesus will no longer work signs for people who refuse to believe. He will reveal to his disciples what the Father has given him (12:50).

The Book of Glory

John opens his account of the final sign of cross-resurrection with the action that takes place at the Last Supper (13:1-30). He comments on the mental attitude of Jesus: "Knowing that the hour for him to pass from this world to the Father had come, and loving his own in the world, Jesus loved them to the limit" (13:1). "Limit" translates the Greek word "end/goal," chosen because it works on two levels. Jesus loves right up to the physical giving of his life on the cross. Jesus also loves with limitless affection, symbolized by the washing of the disciples' feet. That act is the only event John records at the Last Supper, alluding to the Eucharist in the multiplying of the loaves and fishes (see 6:48-58). If the Eucharist is the mystery of faith, much more the incarnation. The Word stripped away glory to become involved in the lowliness of the human condition. In the foot washing, Jesus stripped himself and became model of service for his disciples (13:15-17).

Final Revelations and Prayer of Jesus (13:31-17:26)

For those who have read the Synoptics, John's account of the Last Supper is the most striking difference between the two types of canonical Gospels. Instead of a few verses, John extends this scene to include a long discourse section, which balances the following detailed narrative of the passion and resurrection of Jesus. In structure the two parts make up the last Johannine "sign," but in reverse order, for word comes before deed.

Why has John adopted this format? To affirm that the great sign of the lifting up of the Son of Man, which Jesus predicted would draw all to himself, is also the sign of the Father's glorification (3:14-15). The return of Jesus to the Father by way of the cross is an act of love so powerful that humans are able to believe in God's saving love for them. The mysterious revelations at the Last Supper are ways of explaining what took place by means of the suffering and death of Jesus. Through them believers find life in Jesus (20:31). These discourses were put together over a long period by the school of John to bring to future generations the saving power of the return of Jesus to the glory of the Father. They contain four types of writing: (1) a series of six revelation patterns, (2) a sermon on the true vine, (3) five Paraclete sayings, and (4) a contemplative prayer of Jesus.

The Revelation Pattern Series. John has used the revelation pattern before, that is, the three-part exchange of revelation by Jesus, misunderstanding by interlocutor, and clarification by Jesus. I cited its role in the controversy between Jesus and his opponents (8:31-59). Six of these interchanges occur between 13:31-14:31 and 16:5-33. They spell out the power of the saving death of Jesus for believers who no longer have him in their midst. Believers do not have to be afraid of dangers on earth because Jesus, "the way, the truth and the life," guides them to the Father (14:6). Their tone is consoling and comforting but realistic at the same time. The Twelve will be scattered when Jesus is taken prisoner (16:32). Even in that event Jesus encourages his disciples: "Take heart; I have overcome the world" (16:33).

Jesus, the True Vine (15:1–16:4). In the middle of these revelation patterns the Fourth Gospel inserts a long sermon on the last of the seven I AM titles of Jesus. The vine image is appropriate at the Last Supper where Jesus instituted the Eucharist. The image illustrates the mutual indwelling of Jesus and believers in the context of the grace of Jesus as source of growth. Out of the grace they receive in Jesus, believers are able to fulfill his special command to love one another just as he loved them (15:12).

The Paraclete Sayings. The tension between loyalty to Jesus and the world's hostility was no doubt often experienced by early Christians, who had to defend their faith in a crucified Savior. As the Johannine community reflected on the promise of Jesus that he would not leave them orphans (14:18), they experienced their life in Jesus the vine by the inspirations of the Holy Spirit. Over the years, the Spirit's powerful presence was articulated in a series of five statements known as the "Paraclete sayings." These are scattered throughout the Last Supper discourse material (14:15-17; 14:26; 15:26-27; 16:7-11; 16:13-15). Only in these sayings is the Spirit called the Paraclete, a Greek term that means lawyer or counselor. The term is appropriate for the Gospel of John, which is presented as the cosmic legal trial in which the forces of Satan try to win the hearts of believers away from Jesus. The interior activity of the Paraclete will insure that the faith of the apostles will remain as norm and guide of believers for all time. No distinction exists between the faith of the original followers of Jesus and that of believers of all future ages (16:13-15).

A Contemplative Prayer of Jesus. The final feature of John's account of the words of Jesus at the Last Supper is a long stream-of-consciousness prayer that does not fit into any literary mold. Jesus speaks as one "no longer in the world" (17:11). He is dwelling in the glory of the Father and enjoying the mutual sharing he spoke about earlier in the Gospel. By recalling themes found in his earlier discourses, the prayer forms a summary of the revelation of Jesus. In a sense it balances the prologue, the great hymn about the Word's journey from the Father into the world. Now Jesus is on the journey back and exults in a sense of glory. His prayer celebrates oneness, not only of Jesus and the Father, but of Jesus and all believers in the Father.

The final words of this prayer tie up the entire Last Supper account by returning to the theme of its opening sentence. Jesus, "having loved his own in the world, loved them to the limit" (13:1). That display of love in giving his life was simply the overflow of the love the Father has for Jesus (17:26).

The Passion Narrative (18:1–19:37)

The story of the passion in the Fourth Gospel is a carefully constructed set of dramatic encounters that fall naturally into three parts: (1) the self-witness of Jesus, which opens and closes with allusions to the garden (18:1-27); (2) the trial before Pilate, told in a series of seven scenes (18:28–19:16a); (3) events around the crucifixion (19:16b-37).

The Self-Witness of Jesus (18:1-27). The first part of John's narrative of the passion differs greatly from that of the Synoptics in its omission of the agony scene (see 12:27-30). As Jesus enters the garden, Judas leads a contingent of police to capture him. Jesus confronts the group with the question, "Whom do you seek?" (18:4). Their answer provides Jesus with another opportunity to bear witness to himself as "I AM," the Sinai title (18:5, 6, 8). This revelation causes the police to fall back, and Jesus must give them permission to seize him and lead him to be arraigned by the high priest, Annas. This hearing provides Jesus with a chance to bear witness to the truth. It serves also as the foil for the denials of Peter, which ironically frame the public profession of Jesus.

The Trial Before Pilate (18:28–19:16a). John skillfully arranges the trial before Pilate into seven dramatic scenes. Because the Jewish feast of Passover is about to begin, the Jews cannot enter a Roman court of law (18:28). So Pilate brings out his curial chair as place to render justice. He asks the group about charges. They simply indicate that they want the death penalty, a punishment they cannot impose as an occupied territory.

From this point the scenes alternate between the courtyard and the inner office of Pilate. The scenes between Pilate and Jesus focus on the reality of the kingship of Jesus. Pilate is convinced that Jesus is innocent and wants to release him. But the crowd prefers the revolutionary Barabbas (18:40). Hoping that a whipping will satisfy the crowd, Pilate turns Jesus over to his soldiers. They enjoy mocking Jesus as king by placing a crown of thorns on his head (19:2).

Now the Jewish leaders demand that Jesus be put to death for the blasphemy of making himself "Son of God" (19:7). Startled by the opposition, Pilate once more takes Jesus inside. Jesus puts their roles into perspective by reminding Pilate that the Jewish leaders are using him. Angerly Pilate leads Jesus outside and seats him on the curial chair. John presents this climactic scene as fulfillment of the words of Jesus that he came for a judgment and yet he condemns no one (see 3:19; 8:15; 9:39-41). His accusers condemn themselves.

Events Around the Crucifixion (19:16b-37). John's narrative of the crucifixion is not a chronicle of the death of Jesus. The deliberately chosen details and the four appeals to Scripture to illumine the meaning of events identify this account as the witness of the apostolic Church's faith in the power of the death of Jesus in fulfillment of the Father's saving love in Jesus. First of all, Jesus carries his own cross because he alone is Savior. John pictures Pilate and the Jewish high priests as being on Calvary to witness Jesus dying as "king of the Jews" (19:21). When the execution detail casts dice to decide who will have the seamless cloak of Jesus, the Fourth Gospel records this detail as fulfilling Psalm 22, a lament of a suffering just person.

Only John pictures the mother of Jesus as standing near the cross with the Beloved Disciple. When he sees them, Jesus not only entrusts her into the Beloved Disciple's keeping, but confides him, as model of every disciple, to the protection of his mother, now mother of his community (19:25-27).

Knowing that he has completed the work assigned him by the Father, Jesus voices a longing, "I thirst" (19:28). A soldier understands this cry on the physical level and offers Jesus a sponge dipped in cheap wine and stuck on "hyssop," used in liturgical ceremonies (19:29). Since hyssop was not strong enough to support a sponge, John may have been playing on the similarity of the word for this reed and the term for a soldier's lance.

With a forceful "It is finished," Jesus, in full control, bows his head and "handed over the spirit/breath" (19:30). This phrase is deliberately ambiguous. On one level it means simply that Jesus "gave up the ghost" and breathed his last. But on a deeper level, John says that in dying Jesus "handed over his Spirit" to the Church as he had promised. The quick death of Jesus meant that his legs did not have to be broken. To make sure he was dead, however, a soldier pierced his side. Out poured blood and water, signs of the sacraments by which the death of Jesus continues to nourish believers.

The short account of how Nicodemus asked for the body of Jesus and buried it in a new garden tomb forms the transition to the resurrection narratives (19:38-42).

The Resurrection Gospel (20:1-21:25)

The Fourth Gospel has the same type of postresurrection scenes as the Synoptics—the empty tomb stories and the appearances— for the final element of the shaping principle of gospel, God's vindication of Jesus as his Son. Yet John describes the interaction between Peter and the "disciple Jesus loved" at the tomb. When this disciple sees the carefully placed linen body-covering and the face cloth, "he saw and believed" (20:8). John also portrays the dramatic encounter between Jesus and Mary Magdalen at the tomb. The risen Jesus brings her to faith in the resurrection and then sends her to be the apostle of his glorification "to my brothers" (20:18).

Jesus' appearance to his disciples gathered together takes place on the evening of his resurrection (20:19-23). The commissioning of the disciples is accomplished when Jesus breathes the Holy Spirit into them in a kind of loving kiss. This Johannine Pentecost is in keeping with his depiction of the crucifixion as the glorification of Jesus as king and the beginning of his return to the

Father and the liberation of humans from sin through the giving of his life-giving Spirit (20:22-23).

The Fourth Gospel highlights the danger of unbelief in the doubts of the Apostle Thomas, who was not with the other disciples when Jesus first appeared. Thomas refuses to believe until Jesus returns a week later to evoke the profound act of faith, "My Lord and my God" (20:29).

Many commentators consider the following scenes of the miraculous catch of fish by the disciples in Galilee, the commissioning of Peter as shepherd of the community, and the prediction of his death as an appendix (21:1-19). Yet these events fill out the revelation of Jesus and serve as a fitting finale to John's spiritual Gospel, which reaches out to appeal to a wide segment of humanity. For example, the one title used of Jesus in this section, the address "Lord," employed by the beloved disciple, is absent from the titles in the opening call of witnesses.

The entire Fourth Gospel acts as the final witness of the apostolic Church to the earthly mission of Jesus as Son and Savior. It guides and motivates the believing community to continue to invite all nations to believe "in order that by believing you may have life in the name" of Jesus (20:31).

FOLLOW UP

Readers who are seeking further reflection on individual verses of the Fourth Gospel will find help in Raymond E. Brown, *The Gospel and Epistles of John* (Collegeville: The Liturgical Press, 1988). For greater stress on literary features of this Gospel, consult Robert Kysar, *John's Story of Jesus* (Philadelphia: Fortress, 1984).

Afterword

My hope is that those who have begun their study of the Synoptic Gospels with the help of this guide will feel that they are able to dialogue with these foundational works of the Christian faith. I also hope that this experience will encourage readers to continue their conversation with these revolutionary faith documents and with their hero, the Lord Jesus.

Every reader comes to a book with a variety of personal agenda. These are based on needs, expectations, education, environment, emotions, past experiences. In the term coined by the philosopher C. S. Peirce, we all have many "interpretants." These are tools that enable us to build upon our experiences and to come to a unified approach to existence.

At the end of each chapter I suggest ways to go deeper into the contents of the aspects of the Gospels covered here. These are only a few suggestions among many possible paths readers can pursue. The important step at this point is to continue the journey, to wrestle with the gospel texts and challenges.

Other types of resources for gospel study are also available, for example, audiocassettes and videocassettes. Some of these are recordings of live performances at biblical institutes. Others are prepared professionally for use by groups and individuals.

Personal interest will prove a good guide for the next step. No particular path need be followed. More guidebooks into the territory of gospel study exist than anyone could read in a lifetime. So lack of material is a poor excuse for not going further. True, today books go out of print rapidly. Some of the ones suggested above may no longer be available. Interested readers must consult bookstores, catalogues, and libraries to find what is actually available.

More often than books, magazines can be a practical tool for continuing education in gospel studies. *The Bible Today,* published six times a year by The Liturgical Press, Collegeville, provides updating on individual books of the Bible as well as introductory material and collateral reading.

For those wishing to go deeper into linguistic aspects of the Gospels, I have written *Experiencing the Good News: The New Testament as Communication* (Wilmington, Del.: Michael Glazier, 1984). That book provides more detailed information about the three networks of language, the factors and functions of the speech act, features of religious language, and the workings of religious imagination. All those topics are helpful in becoming a skilled reader of the Synoptic Gospels.

The encouragement and challenge of a group can be an incentive to continue the journey into gospel study. Parish and other groups provide a friendly setting for common pursuit of knowledge and understanding. The gains of research in adult learning make for more active participation in courses.

Deciding on a specific topic or approach and agreeing to deal with it for a limited time enable each group to evaluate its method and progress and to open up to new members on a regular basis.

The value of this introduction will be determined by the habits it encourages in readers: habits of faith, of worship, and of Christian living.

Rereading the Gospels frequently in a prayerful manner is perhaps the best way one can come to appreciate fully the demands of Christian discipleship. These inspired writings assist believers in seeing what is involved in taking up the cross, building Christian community, and reforming one's life. When the Gospels set the agenda for the Christian Church, then the Spirit will renew the face of the earth.